Miracles

Also by Cassandra Eason

A Mother's Instincts
Families Are Forever
The Psychic Power of Children
The Psychic Suburbia
Psychic Families
Discover Your Past Lives
In Loving Memory

CASSANDRA EASON

Miracles

A collection of true stories which prove that miracles do happen

PIATKUS

First published in 1997 by
Judy Piatkus (Publishers) Limited
5 Windmill Street, London W1P 1HF

A catalogue record for this book is
available from the British Library

ISBN 0-7499-1690-7

Edited by Kelly Davis
Designed by Sue Ryall

Set in 11/12½pt Sabon by
Phoenix Photosetting, Chatham
Printed and bound in Great Britain by
Mackays of Chatham PLC, Chatham, Kent

To my children,

Tom, Jade, Jack, Miranda and Bill,

through whose eyes

I have seen a different world

Contents

Introduction

This is a book of miracles that have happened to ordinary men and women from around the world. In many cases there seems no logical explanation why a life should have been saved against seemingly impossible odds or prayers answered when all earthly hope was lost. Even when such 'miracles' are explicable in terms of natural phenomena, the sheer timing and combination of synchronistic factors suggest that life is about much more than the random collision of atoms, that it is deeply influenced by goodness and love both divine and human.

What is a miracle? According to Collins' *Concise Dictionary of the English Language* the word derives from the Latin noun *miraculum* – a wonder. A miracle is defined as 'a marvellous event attributed to a supernatural cause; any amazing or wonderful event and a marvellous example of something e.g. a miracle cure'.

Eminent authorities tend to evade the issue. For example, when a reporter asked Albert Einstein, 'Do you believe in miracles?', he replied, 'What could be more miraculous than a newborn baby?' It is relatively easy to say what is *not* a miracle. But to define the miraculous in a few words or even pages is as difficult as trying to explain love or altruism.

Miracles are easiest to understand not in the abstract, but through their impact on the lives of those who experience them. And so within these pages you will find accounts of miracles from many faiths and from those who profess no formal faith, from the United Kingdom, Europe, the Mediterranean, the United States, Japan, India, Australia, New Zealand and South Africa. Some of the experiences described can be verified by a third party, but their truth and value does not depend upon whether they can be analysed to the satisfaction of those who cannot accept as valid a world too infinite and intangible to be measured with the instruments of science.

I have been impressed by the homely nature of the signs of divine blessing: statues that weep or drink milk in ordinary homes as well as great temples; diseases cured and fertility restored at healing wells in urban settings. These are not the tales of over-fervent or other-worldly devotees, but of practical people who work in offices, shops and factories, our mothers, fathers, colleagues, friends.

A hardened English lorry driver heard what he believed was the voice of God, immediately gave up his well-paid job and has taken more than 55 convoys to the war zones of Eastern Europe. A Japanese teenager rushes home from school to heal the dozens of sick and unhappy waiting at his door. He accepts no money, only flowers which he loves. A housewife from the United States carried her comatose husband on her back for five years. Now he walks, talks and lives a normal life. Those who mocked her are silenced.

Nor do all the miracles have a religious context. A sailor, trapped in a deep under-water cavern after an iceberg collapsed in the Antarctic, somehow discovered the strength to swim through sub-zero waters to rescuers unable to reach him. He believes that it was his own willpower that caused him to survive and this viewpoint is reflected in the book as well as more religious interpretations. Life is miraculous, wonderful and gloriously unpredictable. Love, not reason, is the driving force of the universe, and when life is threatened, or so full of sorrow as to be untenable, a miracle may come to transform that sorrow into joy.

Many lives are touched by miracles. Indeed, perhaps more than half the world's population would define some event in their own lives or those of close family or friends as miraculous. A survey for *Time* magazine in April 1995 found that 69 per cent of Americans questioned believed in miracles. The true percentage of believers round the world is probably much higher. Such belief comes not from blind faith, but from personal encounters with the wondrous. Most families have in their collective history accounts of an escape from potential disaster, a helping hand from an unexpected source when all seemed lost, a recovery from illness against the odds. Miracles only appear rare because too often people are reluctant to share these experiences outside the family circle for fear of ridicule.

My own interest in the subject of miracles began when I escaped unhurt from a North Hollywood hotel that was partially wrecked by the Los Angeles earthquake in January 1994. My escape, less than 10 miles from the epicentre, was not a miracle in the sense of the life and death encounters contained in this book. However my experience made me look at the world in a different way. I was alone, thousands of miles from my children, facing what I was convinced was death. My seemingly secure universe physically crumbled into terrifying blackness. I realised my former belief, that I alone was in control of my destiny, was an illusion. I cried out to God even though I had abandoned Him after my mother's death when I was 19.

Afterwards I wondered why I should have expected a God in whom I no longer believed to answer my prayers. Then I began to collect stories of people who had escaped from almost certain death or disaster, who had been healed from life-threatening illnesses or whose lives had been given inspiration by a vision or sign of blessing they believed came from a divine force. The evidence I have collected suggests that there is something beyond even the greatest psychic and intuitive powers known to be inherent within the human psyche.

However I have also discovered that there are no guarantees of being protected against suffering, sorrow and loss by subscribing to any particular faith; no promises that praying in the darkest hour for anyone out there will bring an answer. Life is dark as well as light, evil as well as good; sometimes even bringing death to the young and totally innocent. In spite of that, every account in the book does reaffirm that prayers can be answered in quite spectacular ways and that signs of being blessed are given to those of many faiths and even in the absence of faith.

I have tried to gather the views of theologians and religious experts from Eastern and Western traditions as well as those of psychologists, doctors and scientists. But expert opinion is included only where it adds insight or offers an alternative view. The real judges of whether an experience is miraculous are firstly those who have known and chosen to share it in this book and secondly those who read the accounts and perhaps find echoes in their own lives or those close to them.

Where possible, I have tried to use the actual words of the people I interviewed. I hope the following pages convey some of their optimism, humanity, and faith in life.

1

A Gift from God

The power of prayer

Christine was 50 and had been married to Dennis for 30 years when, in September 1990, she began complaining of bad headaches that would not go away. By the middle of the week Dennis was so worried he insisted on calling a doctor.

But Christine became worse and on Saturday evening she collapsed in the bathroom. Luckily the doctor was actually in the house at the time and she was rushed to Bolton Hospital. The following morning, suffering from a brain haemorrhage, she was transferred to Hope Hospital for Neurosurgery in Manchester. She survived a five-hour brain operation but lapsed into a deep coma.

Dennis told me what happened:

> I asked the doctor what Christine's chances were and he would not give me any odds. I filled up and up with tears. It was like that for two years, just waiting. The doctors suggested after three to four months of no response that they withdraw treatment and remove my wife's feeding tube. Even if Christine did recover, I was told, which would need a miracle, she would be brain-damaged and crippled and so I should let her go. But I said, 'Only one person can decide whether she will live or die and that is God.'

Inside I was sure Christine would get better, though there was no sign to support my belief. The worst thing was that, day after day, nothing happened. She just lay there. I used to pray day and night, especially when we were on our own. I never lost faith and I knew people all around the world were praying for Christine. Each night I came home and prayed and wept. I used to say to God, 'Either make her live or let her die or let me die instead. Just let there be some change.'

After a couple of months I added what seemed unthinkable, 'Let her be like this if she can just live'. I knew life without her, any life, would be unbearable. I felt angry with God, for my wife was such a lovely woman who never said a harsh word or did a mean deed. Christine was moved to a nursing home near Bolton, since there was no more the hospital could do.

Things became worse. My mother died, I lost my job and had money worries. But even then I did not despair. No one can ever tell me there is not a God. I seemed to come through the difficulties and knew that things would work out. God would not desert us.

Eighteen months after Christine had slipped into a coma, she developed pneumonia. The matron said that Christine had only three days to live. The local priest came to administer the last rites, the Sacrament of the Sick, but a week later Christine was still alive and started to improve slightly.

I used to wet cotton buds and put them to her lips. Christine had lost her swallowing reflex and her lips always seemed dry. At the beginning of 1992, friends gave me some holy water they had brought from Lourdes and I put that on the cotton buds. I became aware that Christine was beginning to swallow and an x-ray confirmed that she could now swallow.

Then Christine started to whisper. Only one or two of us heard her and many people were sceptical. Each night I said three little prayers and told her, 'I'll say the prayers and you think them.' One night, I was saying our three little prayers and halfway through the Hail Mary, Chris-

> tine joined in with a weak voice, the Angelus, at 'Hail Mary, Mother of God', although she was not awake. From that moment, Christine started to improve.
>
> Previously, over the months I had been with Christine, I had noticed that the links on my rosary beads were turning gold. It was not till much later that I heard that at Medjugorje in the former Yugoslavia, where the Virgin Mary regularly appears, rosary beads of pilgrims did sometimes change colour. I do believe Mary did help Christine because they were both mothers.

Christine cannot remember the moment when she joined in the prayer, nor the long months when she was in a coma:

> It's not like the films where a person is instantly awake. It was so slow. I suppose a few months from that point of saying the prayer before I was fully aware. It's hard to realise how bad I was because I feel so well now.

Her recovery, described by her family and doctors as a miracle, was not instantaneous, said Christine. It would have been a neat ending if, after she had joined in the prayer, she had risen from her bed and returned to normality. But real life is much harder and after a miraculous breakthrough can come months of hard work and courage. Christine was given physiotherapy and speech therapy and could eventually answer questions. By Christmas 1992, she came out of the coma fully and began the frustrating task of rehabilitation. She prayed for a normal life once more and by the beginning of 1994 was able to go home. Two years later, she is constantly aware of her blessings:

> Each day is wonderful, a gift from God and precious. When we went to Mass for the first time after my recovery, we lit a few candles and the whole congregation applauded as we entered the church. Their prayers had helped so much.

Now Christine is learning word-processing and French. The couple have been to Canada and celebrated her fifty-fifth birthday in Paris.

The former Chief Medical Officer of Bolton, who has since gone into the Ministry, commented that as a result of Christine's case medical textbooks on comatose patients should be rewritten because her doctors had given no hope, especially as time went on.

Christine and Dennis's experience is miraculous on several counts. Her recovery against all odds could be said to be a medical miracle. Her husband's refusal to abandon his wife on doctors' advice, and to wait for two years without a sign, displays a devotion that is in itself miraculous.

But the miracle remains primarily religious. The rosary beads changing colour can be seen as a miraculous sign of heavenly favour and finally the constant prayer and faith represent the power of prayer to bring about the seemingly impossible.

How can such miracles occur? One answer was given by Dr Kenneth Pargament, of Bowling Green State University, at the 1996 Congress of the American Association for the Advancement of Science:

> Religion offers a response to the human problem of insufficiency. Faced with the insurmountable, the language of the sacred – hope, surrender, forgiveness, serenity, divine purpose – becomes more relevant. Ultimate control is still possible through the sacred when life seems out of control.

~ *Divine intervention* ~

Pauline, a nurse and a doctor's wife, living in Australia, recounted an experience that happened to her while she was living in New Zealand some years ago. She, like Dennis and Christine, attributes the miracle to divine intervention:

> I was sitting in a healing circle that I regularly attended. The group was very loving but I was so tired, as I had

young children who were only three and four years old, and as I half-closed my eyes I almost wished I had stayed at home.

The next thing I knew Jesus was standing in front of me in an area of pure light. There was no ceiling and no floor. Love, pure love, came from him. Jesus had his hands open and his palms uplifted. He wore pure white robes and floated towards me. He came by my side. I asked Him for healing for my father-in-law in Northern Ireland.

For some reason I had been worried about my father-in-law for about 12 hours. The previous night my husband David had a dream and heard his father's Northern Irish brogue call out, 'Hello there', his customary greeting on meeting us. David's parents had promised to come over to see us, but my father-in-law was waiting for a heart bypass operation and so decided to come over to convalesce. There was a waiting list for the operation, however, and David's mother promised to let us know when he was going to be admitted. The dream came at three o'clock in the morning and David and I had prayed all night – we did not know at that moment that my father-in-law had been told of a sudden cancellation and was having the operation.

Indeed I did not know that he had been admitted to hospital until I went home after the healing meeting. Now, as I stood with Jesus beside me, I was praying for the highest healing for my father-in-law, although I did not know why. The brilliant light faded and I found myself falling through blackness, with flashes of colour. I was breathing erratically and I knew I was in shock. It was the same sensation as when I gave birth to my last baby and my body felt cold and heavy. Now, as I struggled for breath, I felt loving hands helping, guiding and reassuring me. Suddenly, I was back with the group being given hot tea. A jacket was put round my shoulders as I was shivering.

The vision of Jesus had occurred at 8.15pm. In New Zealand, we were 12 hours ahead of Northern Ireland.

The surgery that afternoon had gone wrong. My father-in-law was unconscious and had a dangerously high body temperature. My mother-in-law had been warned that he would die and there was no hope. At exactly the moment I had the vision of Jesus, I later discovered, the machine suddenly went haywire and my father-in-law woke up with no temperature whatsoever, to the amazement of the staff in intensive care.

That was eight years ago and he is still alive and well. To me that is a miracle.

~ *Signs of blessing* ~

Some of the most fascinating but potentially controversial miracles which I researched were those where inexplicable natural phenomena seemed to indicate divine intervention or blessing.

I had collected many stories from Catholics of statues of the Virgin Mary throughout the world weeping tears or even blood, but had become embroiled in the inevitable debate over chemical analysis and accusations of fraud and profit-seeking. However I was fortunate to talk personally to a woman who had experienced such signs of divinity and I realised that the real wonder lay not in the issues of DNA and carbon-dating, but what the experiences meant to those who witnessed them and the cures that were triggered by such experiences.

Mary is 80, a retired postmistress who lives in County Wicklow in Ireland. Her statue of the Virgin Mary not only appears to weep but Mary, her daughter and other neighbours and friends have seen the eyes moving and the statue turn in its box. The statue was one of several bought back from the Virgin Mary's shrine at Fatima in Portugal, one of many thousands that are made and distributed, and so claimed no great history or mystical origin. Yet it has become a symbol of hope and faith to pilgrims from around the world who come not to a grotto, surrounded by tourist stalls and media hype, but to an ordinary woman's living room.

Mary told me of her continuing experiences:

I had the statue a while and it had been blessed and used many times in religious ceremonies and for prayer around the neighbourhood. It became a symbol of much holiness and devout love and so I believe it was blessed, though it was a mass-produced statue like many others. On 8 May 1994, I noticed that the statue looked different. The robe was a different blue. I went out and when I returned the whole room in which the statue had been placed was filled with incense.

On 9 May, I did not go to Mass as usual. My daughter was cleaning up and going to do the post office for me. I had gone into the yard when she rushed out, calling me, 'Mum, come in quickly.'

I rushed in and she showed me the statue which was in its box and had red eyes. From the left eye a red liquid was trickling and from the other eye clear liquid like tears. I held the box and saw the statue was really alive. I was not afraid although the eyes were opening and closing and the figure moving. It actually turned in the box. My daughter witnessed it too. My legs went numb and I cried, 'Oh Blessed Mother'.

I knew Our Lady was begging me to help her and that was why she was crying. I had always tried to live a good life and I was distressed by her sorrow and wondered how I could have caused it. I called some of the friends with whom I worship and they came and saw the statue of Our Lady turning and her eyes opening and closing. I sent for the priests but they did not believe me. But they came and saw for themselves and now the parish priest rejoices that our village has been so blessed.

Word spread and people were in and out of the house for days, praying and marvelling. I put the statue on a table in my living room and it continued to weep. Experts accuse me of fraud and demand that the statue is tested. I have never claimed the statue wept blood and I do not want to have it tested. I do not care if it weeps tar, wax, resin or blood. It is a blessed sight and it is a sign that Our Lady is weeping for the sorrows of the world. I have seen its eyes open and felt the statue alive in my hands. Why do I need to prove anything?

All visitors are welcome but I do not seek for anyone to come. I have a home. I have a family. Why should I want more?

People coming to my home have seen wonderful visions. More than 18 months on, the statue still sometimes weeps. The Friday before the bomb went off in London, in February 1996, the statue wept.

I myself have seen visions but I do not talk of them because, as I own the statue, people would say I had an interest. I would not make money from the statue, nor sell it, because it is a blessing, a gift and my sacred duty to care for it and those who come seeking help and guidance from Our Lady.

Many have come and been cured. I turn no one away. People with cancer have been healed by praying to Our Lady as well as people with nerve and drug-related problems. Hyperactive children have become quieter by touching her robe. A man who had suffered a whiplash fracture and was cured of pain, wrote me a letter of thanks.

My home feels like a shrine. The strangest experience concerned a man who had seen an article while he was in a public house in Dublin. He asked the barmaid if he might have the picture of the statue from the *Independent* newspaper. He put it by his bed covered with cellophane to keep it clean. Soon after, he came to see the statue and told me that the eyes on his newspaper cutting moved, as they do on the statue. He had cancer before the experience and wanted to tell me he was getting better.

I am such a happy person now. I do not know why I have been so blessed. You don't have to be on your knees before Our Lady. You just have to know and love her. I feel 20 years younger and I am surrounded by the love of my family and the privilege of owning the statue, a statue like millions of others that are sold at Fatima in

Portugal, that is very special and has bought so much happiness and healing to others.

After the news spread, 500 people a day came to visit the statue. Many have claimed to see it weep or the eyes open and close and many felt a strong aura of peace emanating from it.

Although the manufacturers of the figure explained away the miracle as melted resin, Mary is convinced that the tears were genuine for, as she points out, although many other such statues had been sold in her area alone and kept in similar home environments, none has wept or moved. Mary is a kind, sincere woman who has not made money out of these extraordinary events. Indeed, those whose homes become shrines often end up out of pocket, making tea for visitors and offering hospitality. Logic cannot explain away the power of such simple shrines to divinity. Perhaps miracles *can* begin at home.

Other faiths, too, recognise signs of blessing. The 'Milk Miracle', which occurred all over the world simultaneously on 21 September 1995 was said by the *Guardian* newspaper to be 'the first example of global religious fervour propagated by mass telecommunications'. Millions of Hindus throughout the world went to the temples and India almost came to a standstill as statues of Ganesh, Shiva and other deities were said to be accepting milk. (This phenomenon is fully described in Chapter Five.) But the most fascinating and believable stories of this simultaneous global expression of divine blessing come not from the temples but from private homes where the statues had personal as well as ceremonial significance.

Ten thousand people visited the Vishwa Hindu Temple in Southall, West London, where the white marble statue of Nandi, Shiva's sacred mount, was said to be accepting milk. But only a few hundred yards away, in the home of Asha and Anil who had came to Britain from Uganda, a small clay statue which is normally kept in a miniature temple in a downstairs bedroom also began to accept milk. Before long devotees crowded their small suburban living room chanting praises to Lord Shiva, Hindu god of destruction and reincarnation. They waited patiently to offer the painted statue of Ganesh, which stood in the fireplace, teaspoons of milk.

It sounded far-fetched until I talked to Asha, an intelligent, sincere woman, who described how her home became a shrine for many:

> When I came in from work, my mother told me that the statues in temples all over the world were drinking milk. I had a statue of Ganesh the elephant-headed god in my own little private temple in my house. Ganesh is used on all happy occasions such as marriages. I left a bowl of milk in front of him but my mother told me I must feed him with a spoon. I held up a spoon of milk near his tusk and it disappeared. In the next three days, he consumed nine to ten pints of milk.
>
> My relatives told the wonderful news to those who were waiting to go to the main temple which is also in our road, a few doors away, and soon people were queuing to offer milk to my small statue. Some were waiting until three in the morning. My statue is made of clay but when I felt inside it was completely dry and no milk had seeped through.
>
> This continued for about a week and then the statue would accept no more. I still have the statue in my little temple and it is very precious to me because it was blessed by the same miracle that was witnessed by people throughout the world. I believe that in these days, the young do not revere God and the world has moved so far away from religion. That is why the milk miracle happened all over the world, not only in great shrines but modest homes such as my own. That must be the heart of any religion, to make people believe and return once more to faith.

~ *The hand of God* ~

I began researching miracles initially to find out whether the hand of God was behind life and death escapes. Fiona, a Baptist, who lives in Exeter, believes that her miraculous escape was God's way of giving her a chance to put behind her all the unhappiness of her childhood and to make a new independent life. This is her story:

On 8 August 1985, I went canoeing in the Lake District with two companions. We arrived at Fellfoot Park, which is a well-known watersports area on Lake Windermere, around 4pm. We got into the canoes and started paddling about. I was doing surprisingly well for my first time in a canoe. However, about 15 minutes later, my canoe capsized and I had to struggle out of it underwater, feeling very disorientated. One of my companions got out of her canoe to help me and we began swimming to shore, pulling the canoes.

Almost halfway to shore, a speedboat came towards us. The driver mistakenly thought we were in trouble and came right up to us to see if we needed help. Unfortunately, he did not switch off his engine and I was dragged towards the stern of the boat by its wash. The propeller was millimetres from my face and I can still remember the moment, thinking, 'I am going to die.'

At that instant I cried out to God, 'Please don't let me die. I am not ready to die. I'm not ready to die, not yet.'

I knew there were so many aspects of my life that needed putting right and so many things I wanted to do. A split second later, the boat turned and began to move away from me and I was no longer held helpless by the power of the wash. I pushed my legs upwards and used them to propel myself backwards. I recall feeling a slight bump to my right leg but thought nothing of it. It was not until I tried to swim away that I realised I could not use my right leg at all – I was not at that point even sure whether I had a right leg.

I was taken to hospital. My right leg had two gaping wounds, one five inches and the other two inches long where the propeller had sliced into my leg. I needed 100 stitches in all. The consultant told me that I was incredibly lucky to still have a leg because had the propeller gone one inch higher the damage would have been irreversible and my leg would have needed amputation.

To this day, I still marvel that I survived. I believe that God did intervene and that I was given a second chance of life, which I have used. The scarring still runs deep physically and emotionally, though it is more than ten years since the accident. The scars still give problems and I am currently receiving treatment. However, every day I thank God that He saved my life and prevented me from more serious injury. Life is a very precious gift to me now, although I still do not understand how or why I was chosen to see another day.

The next chapter looks at other escapes from almost certain death. In some accounts guardian angels are seen as the source of rescue, in others a telepathic bond of love. Some people believe, however, that the secret simply lies in the strength and endurance of the human spirit.

2

A Cry for Help

Hearing the voice of God

Narrow escapes from death are the most dramatic form of miracle. But whose hand lies behind these interventions? This is a complex issue and the accounts in this chapter offer alternative views. Like Fiona in the previous chapter, some attribute their miraculous escapes to divine protection. Courtney, an art student living in Washington State, USA, is convinced that his guardian angel saved him from almost certain death. While Courtney was still a high school pupil in Oregon, he fell asleep at the wheel of his car. It crashed into a concrete bridge and turned over. Courtney woke on impact, upside down, covered in glass, in darkness on a deserted country road.

Suddenly an urgent voice told him to get out of the car, but Courtney could not find the seat belt release. He panicked, then felt a hand gently helping him to find and press the release button.

Courtney tried to crawl across the crushed ceiling, but was unable to fight his way out of the car. As he cried out for help, he found himself floating outside the car, surrounded by a brilliant light, more dazzling than any he had ever seen. Courtney closed his eyes because the light was so bright.

When he opened them, the radiance had gone. But the danger had not. As he stood in the darkness, stunned, a voice told the teenager to run as fast as he could. Seconds later, the car burst into flames and was completely destroyed. So fierce had been the impact of the crash that the engine had gone through the floor. Courtney, however, escaped with minor cuts and bruises and was able to walk along the road to find help. Most amazing of all, the only spot where the car's ceiling was not completely crushed was the small area where his head had been. Like Courtney, those who saw the wreckage could offer no possible explanation for his survival.

Diane, who lives in Somerset, also believes that divine intervention saved her and her daughter from almost certain death:

> It was on 10 July 1968. I was crippled at the time with an illness and unable to walk. I had a daughter of three and we managed quite well with the various aids I had been given. It had been raining hard all morning but I was not at all anxious. About two o'clock in the afternoon I suddenly heard a male voice I did not recognise, urging me again and again, 'Get your child. Leave everything and get out of the house.'
>
> At first I thought it was my imagination but the voice persisted, its tone increasingly urgent. At last, I could bear the sound no more and phoned for a taxi to take us to my sister's house. That evening, a local river burst its banks and the ground floor of my house was flooded under several feet of water. Had I stayed I would have been trapped with my daughter.
>
> I am convinced that the voice was that of God and that He saved our lives. I have never forgotten the experience and it has convinced me that life has a purpose.

~ *Saving our loved ones* ~

Diane listened to the warning and so she was given an opportunity to save herself and her child. Indeed, a warning is sometimes given not only for our own protection but to allow us to send love and prayers to an absent family member in need. In my book *Psychic Families* (Foulsham, 1995), I told how Judi, who lives in Indiana, fell to her knees and prayed for her son, Corey, who should have been at school but had truanted and was about to crash a borrowed motorcycle.

My research clearly indicates that we are able to transmit strength and protection to close relations and partners, using an unacknowledged power that goes beyond telepathy. It seems that we can intervene on behalf of those we love on a spiritual plane in a way that can actually affect the physical outcome. In many cases, the frightened parent or partner asks God to intervene but sometimes the saving energies are seen by the participants as emanating from the sheer power of human love. I am increasingly coming to realise that the two may not be incompatible.

Grandmothers can, especially with a favourite grandchild to whom they feel bonded, send protection in a way that seems little short of miraculous. Dalma lives in Bristol. She described how she believes she prevented her grandson's death miles away:

> My 15-year-old grandson Lee was going through a difficult phase at home. But he was a lovely lad and we were always very close. One Thursday evening about 7.45pm I knew Lee was in danger. I opened my Bible and saw the phrase 'Snatch them from the fire'. I was afraid Lee was trapped in a fire and so I prayed over and over again, 'Snatch Lee from the fire, Lord'. At last the fear subsided and I knew that the danger had left him.
>
> Next day Lee came to see me. He was desperately upset but would not tell me why. At last he admitted that about the time I had prayed, he was about to get into a car full of joyriding boys. One of them had stolen a car and they were going for a spree. As Lee was climbing into the back seat, a bigger boy came along and pushed my grandson aside. The car went without him. At 8pm the car went out of control and crashed from Clifton Suspension Bridge. The boys in the car were all killed. Lee had seen the accident on the news.

I spoke to Dalma on the sixth anniversary of the crash and she is still convinced her prayers saved Lee. There was no happy ending for the boy who took Lee's place but that does not make Lee's escape any less miraculous in his grandma's eyes.

~ *Trusting the voice* ~

Perhaps then, whether the warning comes from within our own psyche or from a guardian angel, we should learn to trust it. Dale lives in Washington State but her experience happened when she was a teenager in Vermont:

> I had an old car of which I was very proud. One day, I felt very afraid – I knew something bad was going to happen with the car. I told my Mom but she just laughed.
>
> That night I was going to a wedding shower at a house in the mountains for a cousin of mine. I wanted to leave my car at home but there was no room for me in the other car and Mom said I was just panicking for nothing. After the shower, I took a wrong turn and ended up coming down the steep side of the mountain rather than the gradual longer way I had gone up. I was taking it slowly, but suddenly my brakes failed. I put my foot on the floor but nothing happened and the car went faster and faster down the winding mountain road. I just held on to the wheel and prayed to God, though I wasn't particularly religious, to save me.
>
> The road suddenly turned sharply and there was a steep drop ahead. There was only one small gap in the hedge that led into a field on the right of the steep slope, just big enough for a car. I fought with the wheel and made it by an inch into the field where I went wildly over the bumps and at last slowed among the cows. When my family saw the drop the next day, they could not believe how I had missed going over the edge. After that I learned to listen to my warnings.

Dale's premonition had told her not to go out in her car but she had been persuaded to ignore it. Sceptics would say that she was perhaps subconsciously aware that her car needed attention. But such warnings have an immediacy that should not be ignored. The problem is that if we do listen to them, we cannot be sure afterwards that we were right to do so. The lady in my local grocery store was due to drive to a needlework exhibition about 100 miles away with a friend for the weekend, but she was convinced that the car would have a bad crash. There was no logic to this and she was reluctant to let her friend down. However she eventually decided not to go – her friend had also wanted to call off the trip as she, too, had had very bad feelings about it. Perhaps it was better to acknowledge the warning, and live with the uncertainty as to whether the action was justifiable, than to rely on the Divinity intervening at the crucial moment.

Divine intervention or good fortune?

Dr Steve Donnelly, Reader at the Department of Electronic and Electrical Engineering and Associate Director of the Science Research Institute at the University of Salford, feels that miraculous escapes are less a matter of divine intervention than good fortune:

> On the question of miraculous survival, for every person in the world who by incredible good fortune escapes being killed there is another person who by incredible bad fortune, gets struck by lightning, falls out of a tenth-storey window or contracts a rare cancer when only 21 years of age. If the former cases are to be regarded as benevolent manifestations of the paranormal the latter should be interpreted as malevolent manifestations.
>
> If one looks at the totality of the good, bad and indifferent that occurs in the world – man's deeds aside – it is simpler to regard them all as random events in an uncaring universe. In my view, the good and the bad – that is the intentional good and bad that occur – are all due to the acts of mankind. Clearly if you are an atheist in

> Withington General Hospital, and your cancer goes into spontaneous remission, you will either regard it as a tribute to the quality of the medical care or as a random event. If, however, you are a pilgrim at Lourdes or a recent convert to some dubious alternative therapy, your interpretation will be entirely different.

Like Dr Donnelly, Harry attributes his escape to good fortune rather than divine intervention. Whatever the explanation, few people can have been through an experience as dramatic as his. Harry, who now lives in Preston, described the time when he evaded death not once but twice:

> In late 1942, I was serving on HMS *Racehorse*, a destroyer which had just escorted HMS *Victorious* from Greenock to Newport News, Virginia, USA. It had been a horrendous crossing weather-wise and many exposed working parts on the ship had seized up.
>
> Consequently the first full day in harbour was spent getting things ship-shape again. My task was to clean up the high angle range finder director (my action station) which was abaft the bridge and for'ard of the foremast. I was having trouble fixing the clips of the sighting port so, like an idiot, I stood on the guard rail surrounding the director, to get more purchase. Of course this worked, the clip came free and I went over backwards, hurtling towards the iron deck, some 40 feet below. A split second later, a signal halyard rope wrapped around my neck and stopped my fall. I would have hanged myself, but fortunately I had the presence of mind to take the weight with my arms until a shipmate scrambled up the ladder and helped me down.
>
> During the split second that I was free-falling and I knew definitely that this was the end, the following thoughts flashed through my mind, 'How stupid to die in this way. It would not have been so bad being killed in action. At least that would have been a worthwhile sacrifice.' And, as those thoughts flashed through my mind, I either thought or muttered: 'What a bloody way to die.'

After my fall, I spent two days in the sick bay probably suffering from shock. There were burns on my neck from the rope which took about three weeks to heal. But to this day, I still have a small scar on the bridge of my nose which must have occurred as I collided with the mast on my way down.

What has always struck me most about the whole affair was my thoughts as I somersaulted towards what was, I believed, certain death. I had always thought that, when facing the end, a person's life flashed before them, or they thought of their loved ones. My case, however, was exactly as I described. All in all I was extremely lucky to survive and I try to remember this when any setbacks occur in my life. I am now 74, still going strong but I am still not awfully fond of heights.

After a couple of days in the sick bay Harry was back on active service. I asked him how he was able to carry on. He replied:

I suppose that my reaction might be explained in that wartime tragedies or near-misses, as in my case, were treated as more or less the norm. For instance, on our very next voyage after my experience we lost a man overboard during the night and, although the entire ship's company was saddened, the incident was soon forgotten.

~ *Sheer willpower* ~

Human endurance certainly cannot be left out of the equation. Bill, who experienced escape from death in the freezing waters of the Antarctic, believes his own determination to survive was the crucial factor. Now in his early sixties and living in the West Midlands, Bill told me:

I used to be on the Antarctic expeditions in the 1960s. We would leave England in the November and return in May the following year. We worked in conjunction with the British Antarctic Survey Team and used to take civilians on our ship, HMS *Protector*, to collect scientific data. We would go south as far as we could until we froze up and then turn round.

On 17 December 1966 we saw a huge iceberg, bigger than a tall church steeple, 30 metres high. On it were grey seal pups and lots of penguins. The ship was not at anchor but floating among the ice floes. Five of us decided, as we rarely had a chance to step on land away from the heaving deck, to explore the iceberg and take pictures of the seals and penguins. We went in close on a small boat.

Suddenly, as we scrambled over the ice, one of the faces of the iceberg broke away and the rest became unstable. It was already steep but the whole thing tipped over. As it did so, it became steeper and steeper until there was nothing left to hold and I hurtled backwards. Had there been an ice ridge below, I would have been instantly cut into pieces. Instead I landed in the freezing water. Between the icebergs were deep caverns of water and it was into one of these that I fell head first. My companions were luckier and were thrown clear into the open sea. I knew the cards were so stacked against me that I was going to die. My lungs were filled with the icy water. I was starting to go numb. The temperature was like an ice cube. It was like being in a vast freezer. At that moment the iceberg tipped again. I later reflected that it was amazing the shock of the cold water and the fall had not killed me.

With the movement of the iceberg, the rock tipped in the opposite direction and I kicked off from the hole. I came out like a cork. Above me was the clear sky and I was not hurt. The boat could not come in any nearer to rescue me, because of the ice. If I was going to survive I had to swim – if I had the strength. Where did that strength come from? From within me. I wanted to survive. I needed to survive. There was no time for anything but to swim beyond my endurance to the waiting boat where my companions already were, frozen but safe. I was wearing fur clothes that had frozen up and still had my camera.

In total, I was in the water for two minutes, 30 seconds. Had it been another 30 seconds, I would have died. It seemed like a lifetime. When we got back to the ship, we were cut out of our clothes and were like lollipops. But I had to go straight back on duty. My job was to service the helicopters and there were people we had dropped earlier in the day on various rocks to do surveys and it was time for the helicopters to pick them up.

I was ill for two years after and still have problems with my sinuses as a result of plankton which grew inside my head and had to be surgically removed.

When you face certain death by drowning and freezing there are no flashbacks of past life. Instead the feeling is a cold sleep like fatigue, but what overrides that is the desire for survival and immense internal energies can be raised, possibly with help from the Almighty. Who knows where the power comes from? The report of our escape in *La Plata News* at Montevideo, our first port of call after the accident, attributed our survival to a miraculous act of God. But I still think that there is an element of luck that I survived when I should not have. Had I not escaped, my body would never have been found. Whether it is the Almighty that gave me the strength I do not know, but I have yet to be converted. I think in active service, where one constantly faces danger, one cannot get too religious – you have to rely on yourself. It is a hostile environment which breeds self-sufficiency.

I do believe man has terrific inner strength to overcome illness and grief. It is not something that is handed out but that you develop. I have also been involved in an air crash and two helicopter crashes and have lived to tell the tale. I left the Service in 1974 after 23 years.

~ *Beyond the bounds of possibility* ~

Perhaps the most amazing escapes involving human endurance occur after earthquakes when all hope of finding survivors has been abandoned. It is difficult to draw the line between human endurance and divine intervention, but the two cases described below both suggest a supernatural input. In 1992, in the Philippine earthquake, Pedrito Dy, a 27-year-old fitness instructor, was trapped for 14 days in the rubble of a hotel in the Baguio mountains. He had been in the basement gym of the hotel and was eventually found buried under a mass of barbells and other weightlifting equipment. By shouting, he made contact with four other people lying by him but, as the days passed, they died. Pedrito believed that he would inevitably suffer the same fate and so attempted to end his sufferings by beating his head on surrounding concrete and by trying to stop breathing. But, he believes, he was saved by divine intervention.

Pedrito told rescuers: 'I lost hope several times. I waited for death to come, but when the despair was at its greatest, a vision of the Virgin Mary would appear and she would console me.'

Physical explanations for the visions – weakness and lack of nourishment leading to hallucinations – have been put forward. Yet Pedrito alone survived and was given courage and consolation by his visions. The fact that physical explanations can be offered should not detract from the significance of such experiences.

The Reverend Tom Willis, an expert on the paranormal and religious phenomena, commented:

> God works in a physical way, for example that the wind drove the Red Sea apart so that the Israelites might cross. It was a physical phenomenon but the miracle was that it happened in answer to a need when the Israelites were trapped. Miracles happen in response to prayer, spoken or unspoken, and the fact that they use physical phenomena makes it more not less wonderful. There may be a natural explanation but that does not detract from the meaning of the phenomena to those who prayed and were answered. For those who are afraid of the spiritual world, miracles are a threat to the safe universe they have ordered and so they prefer to do without miracles.

A lack of food and water may then have made Pedrito see visions – indeed mystics from time immemorial have used sensory deprivation as a means of accessing deeper levels of consciousness. But those who do survive when hope is lost are frequently given the will to endure suffering beyond normal limits by a sign of blessing.

~ *Seeking the life force* ~

On 16 July 1995, Park Seung-hyun, a 19-year-old sales assistant, was found alive in the remains of a five-storey shopping mall in Seoul, South Korea, which had collapsed. The girl survived after being buried alive for 16 days without food or water. Dr Kim Sei-yong who examined her commented: 'I do not understand how she could make it. Textbook knowledge says that a human being cannot last for more than a week without water.'

Alistair Wilson, an injury specialist at the Royal London Hospital, said: 'This is extraordinary but every once in a while you find people who are amazingly resistant.'

But Park's father preferred a less mundane explanation: 'I thought I would be lucky to have her remains returned to me. But what I have here is a miracle. Heaven must have helped her.'

A total of 501 people died when the busy five-floor wing of the Sampoong Department Store collapsed just before 6pm on 30 June, trapping 1,500 shoppers. Other people were also found after many days without food and water. Where modern methods of detection failed to find them, an ancient, little-understood mystical art, called *Ki*, succeeded. *Ki*, or *Qi* as it is called in China, is the life force, a spiritual energy that can be felt and seen as heat and radiance. When a person dies, the source of energy that comes from the balanced interaction of yang and yin ceases. This energy can be sensed and seen by those versed in its laws. A respected elderly expert in *Ki*, Lim Kyong-taek, Professor of Political Science at Mokpo University, told rescuers that a young man was still alive in the rubble.

Professor Lim, standing silently on the site, pinpointed the most unlikely place for a survivor – the centre of the rubble – and said a piece of heavy machinery should be moved. Rescue workers were sceptical when Professor Lim told them a young, healthy man, possibly a sportsman, was alive there and emitting *ki*.

At first no one was found, and Professor Lim left the site, muttering: 'It is strange.' But 12 hours later, Choi Myun-suk, who is 21, was found at the precise spot the Professor had indicated.

When another survivor, Yi Ji-hwan, 19, was dug out of the rubble miraculously alive, at another spot Professor Lim had indicated, relations and television stations started taking notice.

Local television filmed ashen-faced relatives showing photographs of the missing, some of them small children, to Ki experts at a nearby hall where hundreds were camped awaiting news. As a result rescuers began to rely not only on sophisticated military detection equipment but also on the life-force experts and it is estimated that far more survivors were found than would otherwise have been discovered.

Dr Donnelly comments on cases of human endurance:

> As far as specific cases of survival in collapsed buildings or elsewhere are concerned, these would have to be considered case by case but there are many experiences of survival for long periods without food, for example in mountaineering accidents, where there have been no suggestions of miracles. Human beings can survive for extraordinarily long periods without food, although this is true to a much lesser extent without water.
>
> I do not believe there is reliable evidence that necessitates a belief in miracles or divine or paranormal signs, but I can be as deeply affected as anyone else by a glorious sunrise, an unselfish human act or by loss or grief. Ultimately, we are all entitled to our own interpretation of facts and anecdotes. I just try to apply the principles of Occam's Razor, which is essentially not to use complex explanations of events that can be explained much more simply.

~ *Talking to the animals* ~

Strangest of all are those escapes where animals are involved. We do not understand the extent of animal spirituality or of our ability to communicate telepathically with them. Anna Chen, who runs a dance company, believes that deep spiritual communication with a wild animal saved her life. I met her while she was performing part of her new show on a cable television station:

> I was 17 and was working in a pub on Exmoor during the 1970s. The owner had a half-tame puma whom he displayed to attract visitors. One day I was posing for publicity shots with the puma. I was wearing a cat suit and the puma was lying on its side with its belly exposed. I decided to kneel up when one of the camera crew dropped a lead and frightened the animal. Because I was kneeling, the puma saw this as a threat, sprang to its feet and snarling, pinned me down.
>
> I could see the camera crew rushing for broom handles and billiard cues and I realised that if they approached the puma it would almost certainly respond to the further threat by savaging and even killing me.
>
> I was petrified but in that instant I became icy calm and quietly told everyone to back away. The claws were pressing through the PVC of my suit and I could feel the creature's breath. I relaxed in spite of this and eased myself to the ground, conveying pure love and submission to the animal in my mind, slowly, gently, contacting and reassuring him. I knew he could read my thoughts. I could feel the strength of thought between us, the unspoken question, of whether I should live or die, his mind and mine as one, on a deep, almost primaeval level, and between us there passed understanding and love that excluded everyone and everything else. Everything was in slow motion – it had seemed hours but in reality was probably not more than a minute or two that I lay trapped. Inch by inch, the puma relaxed, loosened his

grip, scratched his razor claws against the wooden floor and very slowly padded off.

The puma was kept in the sauna and the locals were worried about what would happen if it ever escaped. One day the owner of the puma moved without any notice, leaving no address. The animal disappeared too. Shortly afterwards sightings began of the beast of Exmoor. I am convinced he was the animal who had spared me.

Anna was spared by what seemed a conscious decision by the creature. Perhaps the altruism and spirituality of animals is underestimated. For example, in March 1996, a brief item in the *Daily Telegraph* reported that a sheepdog had saved its owner from freezing to death as he lay unconscious in Hartsholme Park, Lincoln, in bitterly cold weather after hitting his head on a branch. Kevin, aged 60, was unconscious for ten hours before being found. When he came round, his dog, Shep, was lying on top of him, providing life-saving warmth. Sceptics can argue that this was part of the dog's training and that over the years it had learned devotion to its master. But what if the dog has no relationship at all with the victim? In the same month Josh, a ten-year-old Down's Syndrome child from Casaville, Missouri, was saved from almost certain death from exposure by the care of two wild dogs who kept him warm and safe after he wandered from his remote country home in freezing temperatures.

After 72 hours, during which the surrounding woodlands and hills were searched in vain, a rescuer who became detached from the main party was led by his horse towards the call of the wild dogs. The dogs' fierce barking then guided 49-year-old Oscar Neil up a mountainside, where the dogs allowed him to pick up the semi-conscious child and take him on his horse to safety.

The dogs had kept the little boy warm by lying with him. Mr Neil described how he found Josh:

I was lost myself and tried to get the horse to go one way but she insisted on leading me another. The horse quickened her step and then pricked up her ears and stopped, listening. She set off in the direction of whatever she heard. We went a mile further and then I heard the dogs too.

They came running off the mountainside, barking at me. The more I went up the hill, the more ferocious they became. I saw a boy lying down and the big dog was barking at me as if to say, 'Don't you hurt him.'

When I got off the horse, the dogs became quiet. I guess they realised I meant no harm. The big dog was watching from a distance and the little dog was circling round and round. I said Josh's name two or three times and he opened his eyes and raised his head. Josh had spent so long with the dogs, he even smelled a little of them.

I guess the dogs bonded with him and took it on themselves to save him. If it wasn't for them, he would have been dead. It's a miracle that he got a second chance.

Josh suffered mild frostbite but soon recovered in hospital. One of the dogs was caught and was adopted by Josh's family. It was speculated that the two dogs, a dachshund mix and a sheepdog, might have visited Josh's home and been secretly fed by the little boy, who loved animals.

Protection from disaster comes in many forms, but a common factor seems to be love, whether human, divine or animal, or a saving grace from a more abstract universal well of goodness.

Many people experience narrow escapes in their daily lives but in wartime the threat of death is ever-present. At such times these reserves of spiritual goodness are even more vital to counteract the suffering men inflict upon each other. The stories in the next chapter show how war not only brings out the worst in people but can also bring out the best.

3

In Time of War

Those involved in war tend to experience more than their share of miracles, and the vast majority of such wartime experiences involve escapes from almost certain death. The 'how' of such miracles provides accounts of courage and feats of endurance that would not be out of place in any book of adventure stories, except that they are all real-life experiences described by the people involved, often witnessed by others and usually meticulously recorded. The 'why' is more complex. Whether they show the hand of God at work, whether these miracles are wondrous *per se*, or whether they say more of human bravery and selflessness – these questions as old as the universe remain unresolved. The more I research these extraordinary events, the more I realise that perhaps there are no real answers. Why should certain people survive the most horrendous accidents, while others are wiped out? Why should one man suddenly be pulled out of a draft by the stroke of a pen and his replacement be killed almost instantly?

Why look at wartime miracles at all? Because the theatre of war strips back the trappings of civilisation, the assurances of daily, predictable routine and a world where we can close the curtains at dusk and ignore the darkness outside. Instead, loyalty to comrades, altruism and heroism become the stuff of daily life. When every day could be the last – and some of those who share their experiences in this chapter have faced death not once but several times – then miracles are thrown into sharper relief. In wartime, those who experience being plucked from the jaws of death face danger again almost at once.

They may not show any overt sign of life transformation or gratitude to God, but they still possess a deep spirituality that expresses itself time and again in the continuing practical service of mankind. All the former service personnel with whom I have communicated have displayed in their actions as much as their words a deep love of humanity and a willingness to sacrifice their own lives for peace. I was a teenager in the 1960s, born just after the war, and so until I had contact with servicemen I had little idea of the realities of war. In marching with my CND badge for a brief period, I failed to appreciate how many lives had been laid down so that I could be free to protest.

~ *Living with death* ~

Denis, who lives in Totnes in Devon, writes:

> I am 77 but I can still remember quite vividly a life-saving event in Malta in 1941. After a bombing raid on the aerodrome at Luga, a search party was made up to look for bomb holes and unexploded bombs. This was some months after I had flown off the *Ark Royal*, delivering new Hurricanes to Takail Aerodrome for 261 Squadron. Bomb-clearing missions were not looked upon at that time as more dangerous than any other, except that you were out in the unprotected landing area and vulnerable to a low-flying enemy attack as you worked.
>
> I still remember being late to join the group, so I was jogging some 100 yards behind the airmen and catching up on them, to where we were to carry out the bomb disposal exercise. As I reached them, my leader suddenly shouted. What he said I could not hear but the urgency in his voice was unmistakable. We all dived for cover which of course did not exist, so we buried ourselves as

best we could. There appeared no sign of danger. Seconds later, a buried bomb exploded.

The noise was horrific and then nothing. It was an anti-climax of silence and lots of dust. My mind raced with thoughts: How many dead? Was Wingco OK? The Wing Commander had been ahead of the line of airmen and therefore close to the explosion. We all brushed the dust from where we had been lying and wondered what he would do or say. He just took us all back to the Readiness Hut and as we walked I asked him. 'Why did you shout out, sir?' His reply was 'I don't know.'

We were all strangers to one another and the matter was never discussed. Life on Malta was a hazard 24 hours of the day and a shout before a death-dealing bomb exploded was accepted at the time as part of the day's work in war. It sounds blasé to write that now, but we were living cheek by jowl with death every moment. For instance, I once bailed out when I had less than 500 feet to go, when the minimum height for a safe landing is 1,000 feet. Later, in complete darkness, on a take-off that went wrong, I again had to bail out, this time at less than 300 feet. The odds for survival at such heights are also very slight so it would be fair to imply I had miraculous escapes both times.

Escaping from the bomb was equally miraculous. The definition of a miracle I accept is an event inexplicable by natural laws and therefore ascribed to divine or supernatural action.

The explosion was presumably triggered by some vibration and explicable in itself. The Wingco's shout was inexplicable to him, but could be attributed to intervention by a greater intelligence. In the case of the Wing Commander, he acted as a medium who predicted an event seconds before it happened, vital seconds that saved our lives. For, beyond doubt, his action saved all our lives.

Denis attributed the warning of the bomb to a greater intelligence, acting through the voice of the Wing Commander. Just as miracles become a part of the daily life-and-death struggle, so divine intervention is accepted as a life-line in war without the questioning and doubts that sometimes accompany peacetime miracles.

~ *There but for the grace of God …* ~

Richard described a wartime escape in South Africa that he believed was prompted by divine intervention. For him, God was definitely the instrument of salvation:

> I was serving as a DEMS gunner on the SS *Ascanius*. At the end of November 1942, it went into dry dock in Durban. On the night of 1 December 1942, I was returning to the ship after a spell ashore. Apart from an occasional masked street light, a strict black-out was observed in the dock area. This night it was raining fairly hard, and as it had been a long walk from town, I was keen to get back on board. I had little difficulty in finding the entrance to the dock in spite of the black-out because the gate-keeper had not bothered to cover the window of his hut and I could see the light of his lamp.
>
> The dry dock was quite large and could hold two ships. Astern of the *Ascanius* was a Norwegian tanker. The depth of the dry dock was approximately 30 feet and between the ships was a narrow wooden footbridge which we had to cross to get to the gangways of our ships. There was no guard rail around the sides of the dry dock.
>
> Once inside the dry dock location, the whole area was completely blacked out so I had no idea where the footbridge was. I asked the gate-keeper how I could safely reach the ship and he assured me that there was a sentry at the footbridge, who every so often would shine a torch for a few seconds to mark the way. Just then the sentry lit his torch and turned it off, as I started in his direction. I was wet through and tired so stepped out at a fair pace for the footbridge. It seemed that I had only been walking for a short while when suddenly I became

very scared. I was shaking all over with fear and my feet felt as if they were clamped in a vice. Try as I might, I could not put one foot in front of the other. I had no idea why I was so frightened but there was no way I could move.

How long I stood there, I have no idea but suddenly the sentry shone his torch again. By its light I could see that the bridge was about 10 feet to my left and that both my feet were literally on the edge of the dry dock. Instantly my fear left me and I called out to the sentry to keep the light on. I made my way over the bridge and on to the *Ascanius*.

About six hours later, I was woken to go on watch and the MRA man who woke me told me that the Chief Steward's Writer had just been found dead, lying in the anchor shackles. The Steward's Writer who was about my age, 20, told me a few days before he was killed that, with the exception of his brother, all his family had been killed in an air raid. His brother was a soldier, at that time serving in North Africa. If his brother survived the war, I remembered thinking, he must have come back to a terribly lonely life. The Steward's Writer had fallen over the edge of the dry dock in the black-out. I am convinced that it was divine intervention that saved me from joining him.

You ask if I have ever felt I had a guardian angel – looking back on past events I think I must have. Here are a few of the incidents that would make it seem so.

While in a South African army base in Durban, I met Knut, a DEMS gunner who had been landed in Durban as a survivor. We teamed up and joined the *Highland Monarch* together. We were both discharged at Avonmouth and from then we went to various shore establishments and still together went on the *Stratheden*, a liner, and were eventually put ashore in Bombay. It was very unusual for DEMS ratings to strike up long friendships because we were so often split up to go our different ways on various ships.

When we reached Bombay, Knut and I decided to keep

together if it was at all possible. I was given a job in the DEMS office and Knut was sent on working parties. I was on good terms with the Petty Officer in charge of the DEMS office. I asked if Knut and I could be drafted together when a ship was available and he agreed. Later another rating asked me if he could join Knut and myself. The PO was none too pleased and as a result cancelled the draft to the Norwegian ship that he had made for Knut and myself.

The ship left Bombay to test its guns. When the 4-inch gun was fired, its breech blew off and took a gunman over the side with it. Most of the remaining gun crew were injured.

The next ship the PO picked for me needed two gunners. It was another Norwegian ship, the *Bebray*. Once again I asked if he would fit the three of us in. The PO was really annoyed now but he did send two gunners in our place.

After the two gunners joined the *Bebray*, there was a massive series of explosions in the docks caused by an ammunition ship blowing up. More than 5,000 people were killed and many more thousands injured. Thirty-two ships were sunk or damaged. The Bombay Fire Brigade lost 66 men who were killed and over 80 more from the Brigade were injured. The initial explosion was registered as an earthquake on a seismograph 1,000 miles away.

My quarters were in a building in the street that led to the docks. Luckily I was inside at the time of the first explosion. I was not even grazed when all the windows blew in. Of the two gunners who were sent on the *Bebray* in our place, one of them was cut in two by the explosion as he was coming down the gangway leaving the ship.

After the explosion the three of us were drafted to the *Sophocles*. In spite of its name it was yet another Norwegian ship. The *Sophocles* eventually arrived in London docks and as I was entitled to a few hours shore leave, I decided to visit some friends who lived in the

East End of London. I caught a bus to the Bakers Arms in Leyton and changed there for a bus going to Clapton via Lea Bridge Road. After waiting a long time with no sign of a bus I decided to walk. I arrived at my destination without a bus passing me. I had only just arrived when the house was rocked by the explosion of a V2 rocket. The rocket had fallen at Lea Bridge railway station, wrecking the station and a bus that had stopped outside. Had I continued waiting I would have been on that bus. In view of these and many other 'near misses' I think that my guardian angel was working overtime on my behalf.

I was religious even before the experience in the dry dock in Durban. Before I joined the Navy, however, I can only remember going to a church service twice in my life and my Sunday school attendance was very sporadic. In spite of this I had a very firm belief in God. Strangely enough, long after this experience while on the *Ascanius* I was on watch after midnight, feeling depressed, because my mind was reliving some of the dangers I had been through. At that point, I was convinced that I would not survive the war. There and then I promised the Lord that if He brought me through to safety, I would make a point of going to church every Sunday.

Some people might think of such a promise as being childish but for me it was real and gave me hope when I needed it. The Lord kept his side of the bargain but sadly I did not. I made a point of ducking out of every church parade I could. After my demob, I would set out for church on a Sunday but always walk past.

One Sunday I was waiting at a bus stop with a friend who was on leave from the RAF. There was a church on the other side of the road and my friend suggested we went in. We did and, apart from occasional illness or holidays, I kept my word at long last and I have never regretted it.

So why was Richard spared by God while another man died at about the same time in almost identical circumstances in the dry dock? Why were his feet not held back from the edge until the light came on? Why was Richard's guardian angel working overtime and not that of the man who replaced him on the *Bebray*, who was cut in half by the explosion at Bombay docks?

The Reverend Tom Willis commented:

> There are no easy answers as to why God saves some and not others. He has to allow freedom of choice and the forces of nature and evil to take their course. Sometimes God warns us but we have moved so far away we do not hear. It is important to listen to warnings from God when they are given and to trust Him. In case of miraculous escapes, God often has a hand and people are protected by an angelic presence, whether seen or unseen.
>
> There was the case of an RAF man who bailed out of his plane and landed in the sea. To his amazement he found the water was shallow and he was on a sandbank and he walked 2 miles to shore. When asked how he had survived, the airman replied that he had landed on the sandbank and walked to safety. But, he was informed, there were no sandbanks in the area. We can only assume divine protection in the absence of any other explanation.

~ *A life-changing experience* ~

Peter, who lives in Hampshire, described his miraculous escape while on active service with the Royal Navy:

> At the time of the incident, I was a 17-year-old junior marine mechanic, a stoker, serving on HMS *Bulwark*, a converted aircraft carrier now a commando carrier. The ship was operating in the Eastern Mediterranean. It was 03:40 hours on 13 March 1964. I had been on watch since midnight and was due a relief at 04:00. My job was looking after K3, a steam turbine generator. It was a

large machine in its own self-contained compartment which looked pretty much like half an empty railway carriage – long, low and not that wide. The machine all but filled it. The compartment was entered by going down a 3-foot square steel trunk which was approximately 35 feet deep, via a vertical ladder, the only way in or out.

I was logging my final set of machine readings at this time. In fact I had a test tube and a small bottle of silver nitrate in my hands for a water test when the condenser exploded. A condenser is a large tank-like structure approximately 6 foot by 4 foot, full of tubes through which sea water was passed. The turbine exhaust steam impinged upon these, was cooled back into water and was reused in the boilers.

I dropped the tube and the bottle. My orderly little spick and span world had in the twinkling of an eye become chaos, the machine a runaway ruin, and steam filled the compartment. It blew me over. I tried to take a breath but the heat I experienced in my chest stopped me taking any more. I should have stayed and tried to stop the machine, but at that age my only thought was OUT. I was at the opposite end of the compartment from the ladder and had to pass the generator to get out. In the middle of this red-hot pea-souper fog, I couldn't see a thing. The boiler pressure was 340 pounds per square inch at 750°F superheated. All around I could hear metal bits hitting the bulkhead. I started running past the generator when my boot caught a loose deck plate and tripped me. I went the length of the compartment on my chest, unknowingly in the murk having slid under a large-bore steam pipe discharging steam, that, had I passed upright, would have almost cut me in half. I groped for the ladder, my lungs fit to burst, but I didn't dare take another breath.

Just as I had put my feet on the lower rungs of the ladder there was another violent explosion. The ship (25,000 tons) shuddered and I was next to the shudder. I don't remember touching the ladder again. I was blown,

> gently it seemed, all the way up the vertical trunk and gently laid alongside the hatch on the deck above, winded and not a little shocked. I remember being on my back. The steam was coming out of the hatch so violently it kept the shape of the hatch, square with rounded corners. Straight up it went until it hit the deck above, spreading out like the mushroom cloud of a nuclear explosion. I was in a mess deck of marines – none of them stirred. I went to the main engine room and reported the accident. No one believed me. Then the lights went from white to red and I was taken seriously.
>
> To this day, I have no explanation how or why I survived. I was in shock for a couple of days – steam seemed to be whistling in one ear and out the other. There was a Board of Enquiry, resulting in a mechanical failure verdict. My friends just took the mickey and the chap who had the job of repairing the machine reckoned it had taken five years off his life.
>
> After a few days I reluctantly went down to the compartment to see the damage. The paint had melted in sheets off the bulkheads, down to the red lead undercoat, hundreds of condenser tubes in heaps, big holes in the plates where angle drives had been blown free, photos of my girlfriend welded together. My plastic mug was now a dinner plate and there was my saviour, the shattered test tube and bottle. I had been accused of sleeping on watch but had dropped them at the time of the first explosion. It still makes me shudder to think how close it was.

I asked Peter about his attitude to religion, in view of his miraculous escape. He replied:

> I did have problems with religion. You might have to fight and possibly die for your Queen and your country. Yet that same Queen was Head of the Church of England which preached 'Thou shalt not kill'. But I did believe a simple truth and still do, that ultimately good overcomes evil. I believed in my mates, the land of my

brothers, and I slept happily in my hammock, 4 inches of filthy water sluicing around the mess deck, certain that my 'oppos' on watch were doing their best, just as I would do my bit when they turned in. That may sound corny, but I have never had friends the like of which I made in the Navy. Problems, situations, I believe, are caused by man and nature. Nature cannot be tamed. There is no power like the sea and you can only go some way to resolve problems made by man.

During my career, I was on several aircraft carriers, in fact the two largest the Navy ever had, *Eagle* and a previous *Ark Royal*. Every ship I was on had fatalities – I sometimes wondered if I was ever coming home, as we were away for two years at a stretch, travelling all around the world. My job on the carrier *Eagle* was very dangerous, some would say suicidal, except that it had to be done and I was trained to do it. I had to mechanically attach an aircraft to the catapult, prior to launch. The planes were all bombed up, engines going full and we had to run in under them as they were moving on to the catapult, flames from exhausts, propellers whirling feet from your head and jet intakes quite capable of sucking you in and swallowing you whole. I was burned once and hit by 22 tons of missile shot. I did that job 3,000 times at least in 18 months.

So it has all changed my life, the way I look at the world, feel and react, a curious mixture of compassion for the underdog but a capacity for aggression if faced with injustice myself. I am incapable of walking by on the other side.

'Why should the effects of wartime miracles be so different from those of peacetime and yet equally powerful?' I asked Peter. He replied:

I am really still a sailor masquerading as a civilian. Quietly proud to have served, remembering friends on Remembrance Sunday. A percentage of society in active service had, for a few years at least, a more concentrated existence and that is, if anything, the thing that sets you apart. I'd do it again, not for the glory. I remember the suffering too. A visit to Ypres in Belgium is food for thought and makes you realise the cost of a freedom the world takes for granted. I think most countries tend to forget the servicemen and women.

Is Peter talking about divinity expressed by his own courage and his concern for his fellow man? Or is that my desire to tidy up wondrous experiences by trying to draw unnecessary conclusions? Like many servicemen, Peter faced death not once but many times. Are some lives charmed or is the protection that of a guardian spirit?

~ *Contact from beyond the grave* ~

Perhaps one of the strangest phenomena of wartime and for me one of the strongest testimonies to survival beyond the grave are the accounts of those lost in war who appear hundreds of miles away at the family home. The soldier, sailor or airman is usually seen by a wife, mother or sibling. Alex, from Essex, described his late mother Kitty's vision:

During the 1914–18 war, my mother, her sister and three brothers all enlisted in the armed forces. Mum and her sister were ambulance drivers in the RFC (RAF) while two of her brothers joined the Sherwood Foresters Regiment and the third the Notts. and Derby Regiment. The brothers were posted to France and were involved in the big push. Mum awoke one night aware that a uniformed figure was standing at the foot of her bed. She called out, asking who it was, for the peak of the military cap shaded the features.

The figure raised a hand to his forehead and, pointing with a finger, said, 'It went through here, Kit.'

The soldier then vanished. Mum was very upset and told the family who asked her who the night apparition had been. At first my mother was perplexed but recalled that the figure had gleaming buttons and a cap badge which shone like a star. So it seemed that the ghostly visitor was one of her brothers who was with the Sherwood Foresters since the uniform of the other regiment had black buttons and cap badge.

Some time later the family were informed that the two brothers in the Sherwood Foresters were missing and then that one was a prisoner of the Germans while the other had been killed.

After the end of the war, Mum met her older brother who had returned from the Sherwood Foresters and asked him what had happened to her other brother, Len. He solemnly raised a hand to his head and pointed to his temple, 'He was shot through here, Kit.'

Telepathic contact

John is a prison officer living in the South of England. He gave me the following account of two wartime telepathic contacts involving his grandfather who served during both world wars:

> In 1917 my grandfather's ship was in the English Channel, coming back into Weymouth. My grandmother was expecting him home that night. She heard him banging on the window and she thought he was messing about. The hammering continued and she grew impatient and shouted down if he didn't come in she would lock him out for the night. The hammering continued and my grandmother went downstairs to the door but there was no one in sight. She locked up and went back to bed.
>
> What she did not know was that at that time my grandfather's ship was torpedoed. The next morning a naval officer came to tell her of the accident, but that her husband was safe. When she pressed for details of how he escaped, the naval officer told my grandmother that her husband had been trapped behind a porthole, hammering the glass to get out until eventually it gave way. It was the exact time she had heard hammering on the window, as her husband later confirmed.

During the Second World War, my grandfather served again, this time as a petty officer in the Navy on the *Latona* and was again torpedoed during the Siege of Tobruk Harbour in North Africa. He was off watch in the shower at the time and so had no clothing when he was picked up in the water. He was quite badly hurt and lost his memory. He was taken to Alexandria Hospital. Gran was informed that her husband was dead but my grandmother refused to believe the news as she had seen his head appear at the foot of her bed on the night he went missing, telling her he was all right.

The family went into mourning and ostracised my grandmother but she kept faith through 13 months until my grandfather turned up in the Royal Hospital at Hasler, to which he had been transferred, calling her name.

John's grandfather claimed no divine intervention to explain his survival. The miracle, according to his family, lay in the power of family telepathy, that a husband could communicate with his wife as he faced death and perhaps in some strange way receive not only love but the strength to survive. Can it be that death, like birth, is a time when we are so close to other dimensions that we are able to transcend natural physical laws? Do we underestimate the power of human love and the human spirit? Did the refusal to accept his death in some way help to keep him alive?

James, a retired Naval Commander living in Wales, recounted a telepathic link on the point of death, not between husband and wife but between cousins who were as close emotionally as brothers:

My uncles Gilbert [1889–1914] and Paul [1890–1961], having a cluster of sisters both older and younger, grew up as very close friends, almost twins, in a family of nine children.

Gilbert joined the Royal Navy and in 1910 specialised in submarines. After serving in the boats on the China station, he returned to the UK in late 1913 and took over command of the old A7 submarine *Devonport*. On 16

January 1914, the *Devonport* went to sea for local diving trials. Having submerged, she failed to surface and was lost with all hands off Rame Head, Plymouth. The submarine became an official grave.

Paul, meanwhile, tested his vocation working for the Cable and Wireless Company in Gibraltar and at Rodriguez Island in the Indian Ocean. Deciding that this was not for him, he went off in 1913 to learn about planting tobacco on a Dutch plantation in Sumatra.

There one night, he had a vivid dream or apparition in which Gilbert appeared and spoke about a wreck and went on to repeat two or three times, 'I was in that wreck.' Two days later Paul received a cable from his father telling him about Gilbert's death.

I have discovered that adoptive parents, even close friends, have this link. John's mother Kitty, who 'saw' her late brother who had died fighting in France, also saw her friend Maria, who had become a nun, appear in her bedroom. She later discovered that Maria had also died. It is not surprising that people should want to return to those they love in their last moments. As T. S. Eliot said, in *Burnt Norton*, 'Four Quartets', 'Love is itself unmoving, only the cause and end of movement – caught in the form of limitation, between unbeing and being.' In the absence of any other explanation, the power of love, whether earthly or divine, may be as close as we can get to unravelling the mysteries of miracles.

What, in conclusion, can be said about wartime miracles? They are miracles of the human spirit, of heroism and courage, of individual belief and endurance against impossible odds. For some, the hand of God is evidence either overtly or in their gaining a new and deeper awareness of the human condition.

The influence of the divine can be seen not only in life-and-death encounters amid destruction but also in some extraordinary examples of human creativity. The next chapter looks at men and women who have rebuilt their lives, guided by divine inspiration and sheer determination.

4

Divine Inspiration

Great artists and musicians may occasionally claim divine inspiration for their finest creations. However, in my research, I have found that people sometimes receive creative gifts following a bereavement or a major life crisis. They believe their new abilities or direction have been sent from heaven in order to give them a reason to go on living. It is in this area, more than any other, that life-changing, life-enhancing results seem to follow wondrous experiences.

Heavenly music

John, a dentist in his late fifties, living on the Isle Of Wight, claims divine inspiration for his new-found musical talents, discovered after the sudden death of his adult son. From being a man who could barely tap out a few notes on a piano, John believes that he has become the vehicle for profound music, given to him by the Virgin Mary herself.

My meeting with John was in itself synchronistic. I woke with a painful gum and found that it was hard, red and swollen. My present dentist had been away ill and I decided to try to find another emergency practitioner. However, before I could do so, John contacted me because a friend of his had mentioned my name to him some months previously and he felt impelled to contact me on this particular day. He mentioned that he was a dentist and I arranged to visit his home the same evening to hear his story. I intended, if I liked him, to ask if he would treat my abscess.

He told me:

> My first vision came on Easter Sunday, 1986, as I had a cup of tea in bed. In the trees outside my bedroom window was Jesus. I looked again and he was still there. I looked a third time and the vision was gone. I decided to go along to Holy Communion.
>
> The following Easter, I saw Jesus, again in the trees, this time with a beard and thinning hair – he bore a resemblance to my son, Jimmy. In February 1988 Jimmy, an excellent driver who had travelled all over the world by car, was killed on the A1 near Newark. After Jimmy's death I tried to keep busy but I could not keep busy forever. The months blurred into one. It was Thursday, 24 September. I was awake and numb in bed. My wife was asleep beside me. A tube of light came through the wall and hit me. I was travelling ten moons past the moon and then into a tunnel of light. I travelled through the tube with great velocity and blacked out. Perhaps I died and was brought back, for everything was different from that moment, touched with grace and light. When I awoke, I was floating downwards from a great height. The ground was seen as though through a zoom lens – there was an earth path and a walled garden with newly planted conifers and shrubs.
>
> A large patio and a lady sitting on the surrounding low wall, among the rose beds, came into focus. I was mesmerised by a feeling of peace. I've never felt anything like it before. A voice like a benign headmaster's told me, 'This is Mary.'
>
> Mary was within feet of me. I could see the coarse weave of her yellow linen robe, with snags in it. Her head dress was yellow with an inch band of calico, well ironed around her head. I thought, 'My Lady is 2,000 years old and yet she has not a wrinkle on her face' and I was embarrassed by the thought. I said to myself that

they must have sewing machines in heaven because the stitches around the seams of her robe were so regular. She had brown eyes, brown hair and Middle Eastern features. She smiled and the vision was gone. I did not want her to leave me or to lose the wonderful peace that descended.

When I woke, after a glorious sleep, the first since my son's death, the presence was still with me and I heard Mary singing in a high sweet voice, 'Ransom, Ransom, Ransom'.

I was brought up in the Protestant Church of Ireland where there were no crosses and I knew little of the Virgin Mary. My local vicar did not know what the words meant and said I had been dreaming. But I knew it was no dream. The meaning eluded me and distressed my wife as she feared our son was being held to ransom in heaven. Then one day I was walking near Carisbrooke Priory. I decided on impulse to go and see the Sisters who lived there. They told me that Ransom was another name for Mary and was their name for her and put me in touch with the Order of Our Lady of Ransom at Wimbledon.

After the visit, I wrote down on the back of an envelope the words of the song, 'Ransom, Ransom,' that Mary had sung to me. The words sang back to me again in her sweet high voice and I had the music, clear, accurate and quite unlike any I had heard before.

I was shaken, as I was tone deaf. About a month later in my surgery, I heard a second tune with a bell accompaniment and, though I can't usually recall music, I remembered every note clearly. I went to a friend, the music master at Ryde School, sang the two songs for him and he wrote them as music for me. I bought a piano and, using the plastic key guide above, wrote down what I could hear. At the end of the third day, I had my third hymn.

Thereafter lovely tunes came to me everywhere, as I was driving or working in the garden. The words flow or sometimes I hear Mary singing them. Music is the key, of that I am sure, and I feel there is a purpose in the Lady endowing me with this gift. It is like owning a computer but being unable to use it and then suddenly someone opens the files and it all makes sense. My music has been sung in churches and to raise money for the Ransom Accident Trust which I have founded in memory of my son. I now have an electronic organ and have made over 500 recordings. The songs still come unbidden, four or five a week sometimes. I have seen the Lady's hands, crossed above the organ while I am composing, and smelled a lovely fragrance. Each song is like a miracle that comes from beyond me and through me.

I have only heard Our Lady speak once, just over two years after the first experience. She stood at the foot of my bed. 'I am the rose of heaven,' she said and I heard a song, 'I am the rose of heaven, do not forget me', and I wrote it down. I believe the Lady of Ransom has many composers in heaven helping me, for my music ranges over the traditions of many countries and centuries in style. I do not know where the path is leading, only that I who could not sing or write a note of music am daily given songs that I know I must pass on and which must be heard.

John's music seems to have healing powers, not always to cure but to alleviate suffering. He told me of a doctor friend who had a brain tumour, who came to see him:

Earlier that morning, I was making a cup of tea when the kettle slipped and I scalded my left hand with the boiling water. I put it under the tap and there was not even a red mark. When my friend came, I spontaneously touched his head with my left hand and, as I played, he felt the most tremendous surge of healing energy. My friend died, but his doctors could not understand how well he died, coherent, with a minimum of pain and with dignity to the end. His wife decided to become a Christian as a result.

His music has relieved many people's pain, John believes.

As for my abscess, by the next day all the swelling and pain had gone. I didn't book the appointment after all.

Wish-fulfilment, coincidence or divine inspiration? One result of our meeting was that although, initially, I was sceptical of divine inspiration, and I do not generally enjoy music, the beauty of John's music impressed me on a very deep level. John believes that the purpose of his musical gift is yet to be unfolded. But the story is not an entirely happy one. Although performances of John's music have given great consolation and healing to the sick and bereaved, because he has seen visions of the Virgin Mary and claims her as the source of his music, his inspirational songs are not welcomed by the Church of England. Yet, ironically, because he does not wish to leave his present faith, he is not generally welcomed by the Catholic Church either. John asks: 'Who will sing for Mary?'

Dr Peter Fenwick, Consultant Neuropsychiatrist at the Maudsley Hospital in London, the country's foremost expert on near-death experiences who has studied extensively the questions of consciousness and the existence of the soul, commented on divine inspiration:

> I was most interested in your account of a man who, after a vision, was led to transcribe and play music. You ask whether or not this is a miracle or whether there is a scientific explanation for it. I expect a scientific explanation would be something along the lines that he had an experience he never had before and, as this was a musical experience, it raised his interest in music and therefore he started working with music in a way that he had not done before and then this led him to becoming more musical.
>
> However, I feel that this is a rather limited explanation and one just has to argue that, after strong experiences like this, people are different. Certainly in the field of near-death experiences, people can be very different when they come back from their 'journey'.
>
> I very much like the view of the giving of an ability as a compensation for their grief, as this would make a

much nicer world, but if all these things are to occur, the mind has to be non-local and operate beyond the grave.

~ *Heavenly words* ~

Few people are unchanged by sorrow and loss. Ten, even 20 years, after a bereavement or crisis, some are unable or unwilling to re-enter the world on anything but a superficial level. But for others, intense grief and sorrow act as a catalyst for profound spiritual change and growth. Their priorities may alter, material success may lose its importance, and new gifts or challenges can begin to fill the vacuum.

Hannah's son, Mark, was killed in a road accident in November 1984, shortly before his eighteenth birthday. Hannah, who lives in Hampshire, had a forewarning of Mark's death: two dreams which seemed more vivid than dreams, in the second of which she was comforting other people. Indeed, when Mark did die soon afterwards, Hannah remained calm and was able to reassure those around her that death was not the end and that all would be well. The full story is told in my book, *Families Are Forever* (Thorsons, 1993). Shortly after Mark's death, Hannah found herself writing a book of poems dedicated to his memory. She says:

> I do not have any gift for writing. All I did was write down the words that came into my head. Where the inspiration for the poems originated, I do not know but I felt that Mark was impressing me with the words. What I do know is that until that time I had not been capable of such things. It was just like a tape recorder in my head. In fact, I could have done with a rewind or slow-down button at times.

~ *A purpose to fulfil* ~

Do road-to-Damascus conversions occur in the modern world? Not all divine inspiration follows bereavement. It may result from a sudden realisation that one has been following the wrong life path and that one has a new role to fulfil. Like St Paul, Tony heard the voice of God and the mission to which he was ultimately called was no less dangerous. Tony, who is in his early fifties and lives in Canterbury, Kent, was formerly a lorry driver. He never knew his father, a Canadian airman stationed in Britain. Until he was 16, Tony lived in a children's home and then joined the Army, becoming a military policeman. Ten years later he left the Army and for the next 24 years worked as a continental lorry driver. He was married twice but both marriages failed and at 44 he was living in the cab of his lorry. So desperate had he become that he was contemplating suicide.

Tony spoke to me about his sudden salvation from despair:

> I went through the process of trying to kill myself twice. I drove the truck up to 80 miles per hour, fully freighted, on the Paris to Lyons road. I knew a particular large bridge and planned to slam into it. I aimed the truck but twice lost my nerve at the crucial point. I did not have the guts to go through with it.

On 12 May 1988, a month after his unsuccessful suicide attempts, Tony was sitting on Dover seafront, staring out to sea, when someone called his name. There was no one around but Tony heard the voice a second and third time. The voice, which he felt certain was the voice of God, told him: 'Tony, I have given everyone a cross to bear, some heavy, some not so heavy. I will give you the strength to carry other people's crosses and, while you do this, I will carry yours.'

Tony began to cry and continued to cry like a child for two hours. Then he felt two great weights like anvils being lifted from his shoulders. A patch of blue broke through the grey skies and Tony, who had described himself in his Army days as 'a bit of a tough nut', thought: 'Hello, God.' His new life began at that moment.

'I stopped crying and went over to the phone box, called my boss and handed in my notice there and then. I knew what I no longer wanted. From that day, I have never doubted the voice or that I had a purpose to fulfil.'

For a time Tony worked in a hospital as a porter and also as a volunteer Samaritan, helping others who were as desperate as he had been. He married Valerie a year after the experience and since then they have worked together to help orphaned children and those whose lives have been shattered by war.

Valerie told me:

> We started to travel to Romania with our car and a trailer full of aid that Tony had collected from the local churches and people around. I work full-time to pay the mortgage and keep the home running. Tony works constantly for the charity, collecting aid and taking regular 'Convoys of Hope', as the charity is called. He has made 55 trips in four years, first to Romania to relieve the orphans, then to Croatia, Bosnia, Hercegovina and the Ukraine, wherever the need arises, sometimes alone or with me, sometimes as part of a convoy. Each month during 1995, Tony has made the overland journey to Croatia and Bosnia and has promised to take four convoys to the Ukraine each year for the next ten years to visit the hospitals and orphanages to help children suffering from the Chernobyl nuclear disaster.

Valerie continued: 'Some time after Tony had heard the voice, we went to Glastonbury for the weekend and on the Sunday Tony saw a book about Sai Baba, an Indian holy man who is said to be the reincarnation of Krishna and the incarnation of God himself on earth.'

Tony remembered the moment as vividly, if less poetically, than Valerie:

> The book fell off the shelf on to my head, knocking my glasses flying. It was *Sai Baba, Embodiment of Love* by Peggy Mason. I thought it looked like a cook book, but I took it home anyway.
>
> On the Monday a cardboard tube arrived through the

post. It contained a donation from a man called Bhupendra Desai, an artist who lived in the West Midlands. With his cheque, he enclosed a calendar for us that he had painted – it was the same picture of Sai Baba as was on the book. On Wednesday the phone rang and it was a lady who came from Kent, offering a donation for the next aid run and asking to whom she should make out the cheque. I asked her name and she said it was Peggy Mason. I then asked if she was the same lady who had written the book about Sai Baba – she was.

Until that week we had never heard of Baba. I read the book and realised that Sai Baba calls the most unlikely people to aid the needy throughout the world, and the next day Val and I went to see Peggy. In the following October, we went to India to Sai Baba's ashram. I was planning a grand convoy of 100 vehicles and was looking for some sign. However, when I saw Sai Baba in the flesh I felt nothing. We had been 24 hours on a train and two hours risking life and limb with a mad taxi driver and there was nothing. On the fifth day, I was in the *darshan* [holy meeting] and Sai Baba stopped in front of me and stared into my eyes. Tears poured down my cheeks as they had done on the seafront and I felt the most incredible power of love. No matter where Sai Baba was after that I could shut my eyes and feel his energy. On 13 October, Val and I were granted a private interview. He asked me, 'What do you want?'

I replied 'Your blessing.'

He placed three fingers on my forehead and blessed me. Then, although there were hundreds of thousands of people at the ashram and he should not have known us from Adam, he said, 'You go to the countries of war.'

'How do you know?' I asked.

'I know you want to go with 100 vehicles.'

Since then, I have felt constantly protected. No matter how many vehicles go on the convoys, they are all under this umbrella of protection. On one occasion, I was driving alone from Dubrovnik. All the garages were shut. It was Sunday and a public holiday and, as I drove further and further, the fuel tank gauge moved towards empty and then beyond it. I said, 'Look Sai Baba, if I'm supposed to be doing your work, I'll need some bloody petrol right now.'

The engine cut out and I coasted round the next corner straight into an open fuel station. I have twice been captured by the Serbs and held with a gun to my head, but I was not afraid. I know I am protected because the work is so urgent.

I have seen the Virgin Mary too. I had been in Gruda near Dubrovnik. It was in February, four years ago. The village had been totally destroyed and the church was also completely destroyed by the Serbs. A nun came out of the church. We did not speak each other's language but I could see her sorrow. She took my hand and led me into the church and into a small room. There was a statue of Joseph, Mary and Jesus. The heads of Joseph and Jesus had been kicked off and smashed. The invaders had gouged out the eyes of the Virgin Mary. Although I am not a Catholic, I was filled with fury against those who had wreaked this destruction. As I left the church, among the rubble was a single yellow rose. I picked it up and gave it to the poor wounded statue.

Two years later, almost to the week, I went to Medjugorje. I was sitting at the back of the church when I felt rather than saw a white light floating up the aisle. I closed my eyes but I could feel the warmth moving towards me. Two hands were placed upon my head in blessing and a little voice said, 'Thank you for the rose.'

I thought, 'If I can be so blessed for the gift of a single rose, how much more can mankind be blessed when they help others in need.' I have also visited and been inspired by Mother Meera, the Hindu avatar in Germany. She never speaks but her wisdom and healing and the visions she inspires are beyond words. I believe I have much to learn from these holy people. I believe in the supreme light all around us, in God and goodness. I believe that light is the answer to all ills, for it drives away darkness in mankind.

> I have been led to work especially with children in the war zones. I sometimes think that it is atonement for the fact that I have not seen my own two children for years and I once paid for a woman to have an abortion that I now believe was murder. If I save 4,500 children in the field, then perhaps I should start to forgive myself. We cannot undo the past but we can transform the future. I believe that Sai Baba and Mother Meera will guide me in God's work whatever that may be, for I have hardly begun. I am not sure if the people in the camps I visit are Bosnians, Muslims or Croats and I don't care.

Whatever psychological explanations could be offered for Tony's instantaneous conversion, the Convoys of Hope provide the evidence of a life once in ruins, and now inspired by divinity. Sai Baba clearly plays a vital role. Indeed, in the course of writing this book, I have come across so many seemingly inexplicable events concerning Sai Baba that I have devoted the whole of Chapter 10 to his miracles.

Like Tony, Louis Blank, a former workaholic salesman, believes he was divinely inspired to overcome his own problems in order to help others. He was suffering from Alzheimer's Disease, a creeping, degenerative condition from which few if any have recovered. It is caused by physical changes in brain tissue, but as yet no underlying reason for its onset, much less a cure, has been identified. Aluminium poisoning, previous severe head injury and perhaps an abnormal gene in chromosome 21 (the same chromosome implicated in Down's Syndrome) have been suggested. Fifteen million people worldwide suffer from Alzheimer's Disease and more than 500,000 Britons.

Rarely it can affect people in their thirties but it is a disease that mainly affects the older population. Ex-President Reagan in the US and Harold Wilson, the former Labour Prime Minister, are just two great figures, ravaged in their later years by this cruel degeneration of intellect and memory.

Louis Blank believes he is the only person in Britain to recover from Alzheimer's Disease, although he says there are several cases in the United States where remission or recovery has taken place and he now offers hope for other sufferers.

Mr Blank, who comes from Rochdale, told me that three specialists had diagnosed him as having Alzheimer's Disease – he had an IQ of 142, but got to the stage where he no longer recognised his daughter in the lift of his own block of flats. At one stage he did not speak for three months and became so incapacitated that he could not feed himself or be left alone. Louis was 53 when his mental faculties began to fail and he became so depressed at his prognosis and deteriorating mental faculties that he twice attempted to commit suicide.

In despair, once the diagnosis had been made, during periods of ever-decreasing lucidity, Louis went to the reference section of Manchester Central Library to see what he could find out about the disease that was slowly destroying his mind. He told me:

> One day, I took three books to a table some distance from the shelf and sat down. All three linked Alzheimer's Disease to aluminium and mercury accumulating in the brain. Then I glanced idly at a fourth book which had been left open on the table and the words on the page leaped out at me. 'Magnesium attaches itself to aluminium and the body will automatically expel magnesium.'
>
> If magnesium attached itself to aluminium, therefore it could be used to expel the aluminium that it seemed was causing the degeneration. It came like a flash of pure inspiration. I had been given the answer.
>
> The bell rang and the library was due to close. I realised the full significance of the experience. I only had three tickets, all of which were in use. The fourth book was already on the table I had chosen, some distance from the medical section, in a place where I did not usually sit. It was open at the right page, waiting to give the answer I had been seeking. I noted the title, *Toxicology*, and made up my mind to return the next day to read the book. But I never could find or trace the book again.
>
> I devised a diet, based on what I had discovered and concentrated on ridding my body of the poisonous metal

toxins. Within weeks of going on a special diet and having my mercury fillings removed, my condition improved dramatically and the only set-back came briefly when I ate a meal that had been cooked in an aluminium saucepan. It was not easy – I had to force my mind hour after hour to remember and to relearn – but from that day I was on the road back to health.

Now I feel that some divine force has pushed me into writing a book to share my discovery and I am giving the royalties to the Alzheimer's Society in gratitude for my cure.

It was never my intention to write a book for general circulation. I produced a home-made book, six copies, about my own experience, and deposited a copy in the local library. I wrote it to prove to the doctors and to myself that I had recovered – previously I had not been able to tell them the day of the week or the name of the current Prime Minister. Shortly afterwards, my local W.H. Smith contacted me, as they had received many enquiries about my book, and I arranged to self-publish the book in paperback. It sold incredibly well and several people have told me they too have benefited from my diet and that their lives have improved beyond measure. I have now brought out the book, *Alzheimer's Challenged and Conquered* (Foulsham, 1996), in hardback commercially.

Two years after writing his first book, Louis is still well, lucid and planning a second title. He knows there are no guarantees for himself or other sufferers but he feels that at least he has been given a chance.

An accident or illness that wipes away the certainties of tomorrow does not necessarily mean the end, but can trigger a determination to survive. Stories of miracle cures abound, and the next chapter looks at some of these and at the incredible ability of the human mind, body and spirit to overcome even the most devastating disease.

5

The Power of Prayer

Medical science finds it hard to explain why some patients with a seemingly hopeless prognosis should go into spontaneous remission or even totally recover. However, behind many clinical 'miracles' lie stories of family prayer. This chapter not only looks at the power of prayer and faith, but at sites of healing, pagan as well as Christian, that seem to contain accumulated curative energies.

Overcoming disease with prayer

Can prayer have an effect in the case of serious illness? Is this power necessarily divine or is it the power of human love that in some scarcely understood way triggers the immune system of the person with whom we are bonded?

Keith, who lives in Milford Haven in Wales, told me about the miracle he believed saved his life more than 50 years ago:

> I come from a family of coalminers, hard-working people, not learned in book terms but very loving. When I was a young lad, I was taken to hospital in the Rhondha Valley, desperately ill with meningitis and diptheria. I was paralysed and in those days there were no drugs to help. My family were told I was dying and that there was no hope.

My grandad refused to leave the hospital, refused to leave me, although the nurses told him there was nothing he could do and it was just a matter of time. Grandad went into a coke house outside the ward, because there was nowhere else he could be alone. He sat in the dark and prayed for me. Suddenly he saw a light in the roof and a voice asked, 'What's the matter, my son? Why are you crying?'

My Grandad replied: 'My grandson is dying and the doctors can't help him. Can you save him?'

The voice told Grandad to have faith and that I would live. 'Go back to your grandson and wait.'

Grandad went back to the ward and insisted he stayed with me, which was unheard of at the time. That night I turned the corner and started to get better. When I left hospital, I was no longer able to read and write but, with Grandad's help, I learned again. I am 56 now and my Grandad is no longer with me. I am convinced he saved my life.

Medical research increasingly suggests that prayer is efficacious in overcoming disease. An American doctor, Randolph Byrd, carried out an experiment in which 200 patients admitted to San Francisco State Hospital with heart attacks were allocated to a group of Christians who said daily prayers on their behalf, with a further 200 similarly afflicted patients as a control group.

Significantly fewer of those who had prayers said on their behalf suffered a stroke or further heart attack while in hospital or died. Dr Byrd concluded that prayers of intercession did have a beneficial therapeutic effect.

For whatever reason, the power of prayer time and again offers hope when all is lost. Johanna, who lives in South Africa, is a firm believer in the power of prayer which she is convinced led Jesus to cure her brother John of a potentially fatal illness. Johanna had an incredibly hard time caring for her sick mother, who eventually died, and her brother, as well as her own family. After her mother's death, Johanna feared she would lose her brother too. Yet her faith did not waver and she continued to pray and ask for help, determined that with God's help he would get better:

> My brother John was becoming weaker every day, losing weight rapidly, and he became so ill he lost the use of his hands, legs and speech. I placed myself in Jesus's hands and used to go round the beds of all the sick people, not just my John's, saying the rosary.
>
> One afternoon, when I arrived at the hospital, I knew that today my prayers would be answered. I dressed my brother warmly and told him. 'This is the day you are going to walk again.' I went with him into the garden, put my two hands under his and, supporting him, moved slowly with him for about ten minutes. It seemed hopeless but I believed that Jesus would help me. At that moment I saw in front of me, not my brother but Jesus's body formed in his. I wept with joy and I had new hope.
>
> From then, every day my brother's strength and health returned until, on the fortieth day, as I entered the hospital, I saw him walking slowly towards me. Six years have passed and John is still cured.

Sceptics say that such improvements in health are caused by belief, rather than by any miraculous powers of prayer. But even science and medicine are coming to recognise that such a simplistic view may ignore the complex relationship between body, mind and soul. Dr Herbert Benson, a Harvard Medical School Professor, has been reported as saying: 'The supposed gulf between science and spirituality in healing does not always exist.'

By repeating prayers, words or sounds, and passively disregarding other thoughts, many people are able to trigger a specific set of physiological changes. According to Dr Benson, 'Invoking prayers or mantras over and over can lower the rate of breathing and brain wave activity, sometimes healing what ails you and averting the need for invasive surgery or expensive medicine.'

Dr Benson, founder of the Mind/Body Medical Institute at

Deaconess Hospital in Boston, started his research about 25 years ago when people practising transcendental meditation asked him to look into its physiological effects. He compiled scientific evidence on the health benefits of transcendental meditation, then began studying how a change in thinking could heal those suffering from stress-related diseases. Prayer was found to be the most efficacious method of bringing about a positive outcome. He sees prayer as part of a three-pronged attack on illness, the other two being medicine and surgery, if necessary.

Further support for this theory was offered at the 1996 Annual Conference of the American Association for the Advancement of Science when Dr Harold Koenig said that 'church-related activity may prevent illness both by a direct effect, using prayer or scripture reading as coping behaviours, as well as by an indirect effect through its influence on health behaviours'.

Dr Dale Matthews, of Georgetown University School of Medicine, reviewed 212 individuals and found that religion had a positive effect in three-quarters of the cases, notably those involving substance abuse, alcoholism, mental illness, quality of life, illness, and survival. 'Whether one looks at cancer, hypertension, heart disease, or physical functioning, most of the studies demonstrate a positive effect,' he said. 'Eight out of ten studies on survival showed that religious people live longer.'

And these results cannot be entirely explained by the generally healthier lifestyle of churchgoers. A study of 4,725 people in Alameda County, California, revealed that on average church members had lower mortality rates than others, irrespective of socio-economic status, smoking, drinking, physical inactivity and obesity.

Another finding was that almost all patients who undergo heart surgery – including atheists – pray. A study of bypass surgery patients showed that the six-month mortality rate was 9 per cent overall, 5 per cent in churchgoers, 12 per cent in those who did not go to church, and zero in the 'deeply religious'.

~ *There is always hope ...* ~

So how long should one pray? In Chapter 1, Denis prayed at his comatose wife's bedside for two years and his prayers were answered. But few can claim to have waited or prayed as long as Gary's family. The miracle actually happened at a time when it looked as though Gary, who had been in a coma for over seven years, might finally die. Medical experts have no real explanation for his dramatic improvement. Gary had been shot in the head by a drunk while working for the police department in Walden, a town near Chattanooga, Tennessee. He had been in a coma since September 1988. Then, in February 1996, Gary suddenly started talking again.

Seriously ill with a 104°F fever and lung infection that had turned into pneumonia, Gary had been transferred from a nursing home to a Chattanooga hospital. Fluid was removed from his lungs and he was treated with antibiotics. When his fever broke, he started to mumble. Then he spoke distinctly to his sister, Lisa.

Lisa described the moment her brother spoke as 'suddenly putting on a light switch in a dark room'. Gary soon began asking questions and telling jokes. He called his mother and brother on the telephone. He asked for his sons, whom he had not seen since they were five and 12.

When the boys, Colt and Sean, now 12 and 20, walked into their father's room, he recognised them instantly. Over the next 18 hours, Gary talked about his horses, his mountain home near Chattanooga and the annual winter camping trips he took with his friends.

While amazed and encouraged by Gary's consciousness, doctors warned the family that the improvement could be temporary. The brain works to repair itself from injury, but how long it could keep Gary alert, they said, was unknown.

Dr Ronald Cranford, a neurologist, said such a dramatic change after such a long time was 'phenomenally rare'. Dr Cranford, of the Hennepin County Medical Center in Minneapolis, also commented: 'Something dramatic did happen in the hospital. There was apparently a marked improvement in his neurological condition soon after hospitalization. I don't know what the trigger was.'

Gary's attending physician, James Folkening, could give no medical explanation for the breakthrough, which the family attributed to divine intervention. But Dr Kaplan, Gary's neurologist, stressed that 'even the reappearance of speech does not change the fact that Gary may continue to be severely neurologically impaired, though it certainly bolsters optimism for further meaningful verbal communication'.

By early March, Gary had been transferred back to a nursing home. Doctors said he no longer required hospital care but he will undergo speech and physical therapy. I have included the story for, whatever the medical situation by the time this book is published, Gary was able to communicate with his loved ones in a meaningful way after years of silence. Medical miracles, more than any other kind, offer no guarantees of permanence. Yet the sudden transformation in Gary's case shows that there is always hope, no matter how bleak the prognosis appears.

Places of healing

One of the most remarkable of such phenomena is the apparent healing power of religious shrines. Throughout the world, often on the site of a reported visitation of the Virgin Mary, such shrines provide a focus for apparently spontaneous healings, perhaps explained by the religious energies accumulated through prayer. Equally, the resting places of quite ordinary men, women and children can be endowed with such collective healing powers, as a result of those who have prayed there for relief. Charlene was only 12 when she died of leukaemia. She was buried in 1959 in a small village in southern central Lousiana in the United States and her grave has become a focus for many seemingly inexplicable healing miracles.

Thousands of sick people come to Charlene's grave each year to ask for healing and for Charlene to intercede with God on their behalf. One case that attracted great media attention, perhaps because the two little girls involved seemed to be linked on a psychic level, was that of Nicole who came from another part of Louisiana. Nicole was very ill with neuroblastoma and was expected to die. In early 1988, weak from chemotherapy, she asked her babysitter to let her talk with a girl called Charlene. Nicole's family thought Charlene was an imaginary friend and placated the sick child, until Nicole's grandmother received a phone call from a lady who had heard of Nicole's illness. The woman had been praying to Charlene for her own grand-daughter's recovery and suggested Nicole's granny did the same.

Nicole's family were put in touch with Father Calais, a priest in Lafayette, who had himself, he believed, received help from Charlene in raising money for the needy. Father Calais drove the family to Charlene's grave. He held Nicole in his arms so that she could see Charlene's picture and Nicole, in spite of her illness, immediately seemed happier and calmer. Soon after visiting the grave of Charlene, Nicole became well and it seems that the cancer, against which she struggled for three years, is gone. There are no guarantees of permanence but Nicole has enjoyed a period of good health. It could also be argued that spontaneous remissions do occur naturally, but the strange link with Charlene suggests that the improvement was not through chance alone.

There have been many other apparently spontaneous remissions and recoveries after prayers at Charlene's grave and these are being documented by the Diocese of Lafayette in an attempt to get the shrine officially recognised. Prayer, belief, accumulated healing energies, all may be implicated at such centres of seemingly miraculous healings. We have no idea of the power of the human spirit as well as mind to bring about restoration of the human body. What we do know is that there are historical precedents in the pagan, as well as the Christian world, for shrines such as Charlene's.

~ *The gift of life* ~

Pilgrims have visited holy wells to pray and drink the healing waters since ancient times, for water has always represented life and health. Many of these holy water sources started as wells dedicated to pagan deities and in areas such as Cornwall the dressing of holy wells with flowers recalls their pre-Christian origins.

One such ancient well on the Isle of Sheppey has legendary healing powers. Originally dedicated to the Celtic Triple Goddess, since its excavation its magical properties seem to have been reawakened. The well used to be inside Minster Abbey, which in ancient times was called Monasterium Sexburga and was founded in 670 by the Queen of Kent, later St Sexburga. This well is now gaining a reputation as a source of fertility.

Although they are not life-threatening, fertility problems blight many lives today. Male fertility is declining, although science does not understand why, and may well continue to do so. Anxiety can prevent conception in couples who have used hormonal contraception until their mid-thirties and found that babies do not come automatically in response to the ticking of the biological clock. The Well of the Triple Goddess, as it is called, claims two 'miracle' babies in cases where carrying a baby to full term, not anxiety, was the problem. Because the well is capped the miraculous powers come from a less tangible source than the water itself.

When the well was excavated in 1990/1991, a pre-Christian fertility symbol was discovered deep in the mud. The metal image was that of a three-headed pregnant woman, relating to the Triple Goddess, who was worshipped as maiden, mother and crone. The discovery of this image implied that the site had been used for pagan worship long before Sexburga's Abbey and, as a pagan water shrine, had been dedicated to the goddess of fertility. The metal image may have been thrown into the well by a rich childless woman or it could have been the original mould for wax fertility images, cast by accident into the waters. This theory is supported by the discovery of fragments of beeswax, also found in the well, that were pieced together to make the same image. The beeswax images may have been for the peasantry.

It seems that the ancient fertility powers have retained their potency since Sharon, a local woman, gave birth to a daughter, Emily, in June 1991, nine months after her archaeologist husband Ian first touched the fertility symbol while excavating the well. In early 1993, Sharon gave birth to a second daughter, Hannah. Previously she had had four miscarriages.

Ian, her husband, told me:

> I would certainly like to believe that the image of the fertility goddess helped us. Sharon had been to see the specialists but they did not know what the problem was. If the image was believed in all those years ago, there must be something in it.

Sharon explained how her despair turned into hope:

> The last miscarriage was at 10–11 weeks and the doctors did not know why. The scan I had at the London Hospital showed that the baby was fine and tests could not reveal why I lost my babies. I had started to feel that I would never have children but I was determined not to give up whatever I had to go through. Ian must have mentioned finding an image but I did not take any special notice because he was always uncovering historical objects and I was totally immersed in the problem of having a child. I almost wish I had known of the magical significance. It would have given me hope.
>
> I almost lost our first daughter, Emily. I started to miscarry with her, as I had with all the babies I had lost. There was no reason at the time why she should have survived when the others did not. Then, on 26 February, our second child, Hannah, was born. The next day, Ian brought home a book that Brian Slade, President of the Sheppey Archaeological Society, had written, *England's Second Glastonbury*, about the local well my husband had excavated. As I read it I realised that Emily had been born nine months after Ian had first touched the image. I have seen the image – it is old and very funny-looking. I would not touch it now, as I do not want any more children. I think it is important since it does offer hope and without that you have nothing.

Brian Slade says that childless couples, who have heard of Sharon and Ian's experiences, have come from as far away as Mexico to touch the Triple Goddess image and ask its blessing. He sees the power of the image as one built up by cumulative prayer in earlier times.

Commenting on the birth of Sharon and Ian's children, he said:

> Ian was one of the first to touch the image. I find it interesting that if the couple had known the significance of the image then the birth of their children could have been explained away as mind over matter. But the fact was that neither of the couple knew its significance. Ian's interest was that of an archaeologist finding a treasure as part of an investigation.
>
> It happened without foreknowledge. I sometimes think that the explanation for such images lies in the powers they unconsciously reawaken in us. If you go back far enough, over the centuries, to the number of pregnant women and those wanting children who visited the shrine and prayed to the goddess of fertility, then a sympathetic energy source is created. When an empathic person comes to Minster, he or she may be influenced by those energies in a physical way.

Certainly those who hold the image feel energies surging from it. Brian believes that there may be a ritual reason for the beeswax fertility images that were also discovered in the well at Minster Abbey. The bees who pollinated the plants were seen in early times as emissaries of the Great Mother. Later the Goddess Demeter was known as the pure Mother Bee. And the priestesses were known as *lissae*, Latin for 'bees'.

One such happening could perhaps be dismissed as coincidence but, in February 1996, Brian told me that as a result of an article in *Fortean Times*, the journal of unexplained phenomena, various donations were sent to enable the well to be opened to the public. 'Among the responses was a cheque for £50 to help pay for the Well of the Triple Goddess to be restored and turned into a tourist attraction and place of pilgrimage,' he said:

> Now that I had raised all the needed money, I was compiling a list of donors to the Well Restoration Fund to be displayed alongside the well and mentioned in associated books, pamphlets, etc. However, I could not read the signature of a particular donor on a £50 cheque, received months before, and so I addressed the letter of thanks to Mr and Mrs – and the address, which I could read. Not wishing to have the £50 cheque donor left off the list, I wrote explaining about the list and asking for the donor's full name. The following letter came back from another Ian who lives in Bedfordshire: 'I am very glad to have my name included in the list of donors, the more so because, after four miscarriages, my wife Maggie gave birth to a healthy little boy last week [February, 1996].
>
> I read about your project in the *Fortean Times* last summer and so you can imagine I was very struck by the story of the other Ian and his wife Sharon. Maggie was in the early stages of pregnancy at the time so it seemed appropriate to make an offering. I've made one other offering and we've both consumed rather a lot of vitamins to see this baby to a successful conclusion, so who knows what got the little one through? Your letter arriving so soon after the birth, however, did come as something of a reminder.
>
> I have just told Maggie about the well and what I'd been spending money on and she was tickled by the whole thing. I am a medical research scientist by profession.

Brian points out that the donation was made as a votive offering in ancient tradition, in the hope that after the miscarriages Maggie would carry a baby to full term. He comments:

> Both husbands were called Ian, both wives had four miscarriages and pagans will note that, like Sharon's second

baby, this 'miracle baby' was born on 26th February. Around this time of year was Bride's Day, an early birth and fertility festival of the goddess of the Well. In the second case, Ian kept his offering quiet from his wife until she had successfully given birth, again suggesting more than mind over matter.

Within the Catholic Church, too, fertility miracles have been reported, again involving a magical object. Sister Chlora, Mother Superior of a convent in Naples, Italy, has a fertility chair that once belonged to Sister Maria Francesca, a nun who lived in the 1700s. She was canonised for miracles, many of which helped women in matters of fertility and childbirth. Thousands of women have visited the convent, sat in the chair and prayed for a child. One of the success stories is that of 32-year-old Giovanna who lives in Naples and gave birth to triplets, after having spent five years trying to get pregnant. Sister Chiara said that few women who have come to pray and sit in the wooden chair have failed to become mothers soon afterwards.

Can fertility be affected by prayer? Dr Julian Walter, of Balcombe in West Sussex, is convinced it can. He was visited by a married couple who had tried fertility treatment without success. They had come to his surgery to ask about adoption. Dr Walter suggested that they might all pray for help. Six weeks after the prayer session, the wife had a positive pregnancy test and subsequently gave birth to a healthy child.

Even the rich and high-born have called on ancient fertility energies. The late Marquess of Bath and his second wife Virginia, whose ancestral home was the famous Longleat House, visited the ancient chalk giant at Cerne Abbas in Dorset in 1958. Many experts believe the 180-foot giant with its 26-foot phallus etched in chalk on the hillside is more than 2,000 years old. The Giant is one of about 50 chalk carvings in Britain and is thought to represent either the god Hercules or a Celtic giant-deity of fertility. The late Marquess and his wife had tried for months to conceive a child and, like countless childless couples who spent the night on the hillside, visited the Giant with positive results. The Marchioness has commented: 'I conceived soon afterwards and we called the child Sylvy Cerne in grateful thanks.'

~ *Healing the spirit* ~

The link between mind, body and spirit is elusive. Praying or visiting a holy shrine may produce no results and it is easy to dismiss the power of prayer in such instances. But some psychologists and healers suggest that, while our own negative feelings may not directly cause illness, they can certainly appear as physical symptoms and prevent even prayer from effecting a cure. Resolving the anger or guilt may, therefore, bring about a 'miracle' cure. So says Ken, a devout Catholic from Crawley, Sussex, who explained how his back was miraculously healed. His sudden recovery raises many questions about the nature of healing – from whence it comes and whether, in some cases, the healing is of the spirit rather than of the body:

> In 1976, I was crippled with a bad back. During the summer holidays I was in such pain that I had to ask my wife to drive the car. My doctor told me that nothing could be done about my pain. Her actual words were: 'You can take aspirin four times a day for the next 20 years or so.'
>
> In the New Year I went with a friend, Jeff, who is now a priest, to a big Catholic Charismatic Conference in Manchester. During the first evening several hundred of us were assembled in the hall to meet our leaders for the week, three American Jesuit priests and a young woman from New York, called Carol-Marie Bandini. They stood on the stage and introduced themselves. Carol-Marie spoke for about three minutes and all that she said was that she was there to talk about personal relationships.
>
> As she spoke, I experienced a sudden conviction that my own relationship with my eldest daughter was all wrong and that the fault was mine. It was like a message from God. If anyone else had said it to my face, I would

have argued fiercely against them. But, for the next day or so, all I wanted to do was to find a priest and confess and tell him what had happened.

Then, halfway through the week, I suddenly realised that I was entirely free from back pain. Normally, continuous sitting would have been agony. I eventually went to confession and told the priest about my conviction and my apparent healing. His reaction was 'Praise God!'

The bad back has never returned, even though my job as a gardener has often involved heavy manual work, digging, lifting heavy weights. I have never tried to explain this healing at all. All I can relate is that up to Carol-Marie's talk, I was near crippled with recurring pain and that, since my sudden conviction, my back has never given me any trouble, beyond the odd temporary pain due to over-exertion.

My feelings are similar to those of the man born blind. In John, Chapter 9, 'All I know is I was blind and now I can see.'

~ *Divine energy and human skill* ~

However, in concentrating on the power of prayer and healing sites, we may end up disregarding the miracles of medical science. When can a natural biological process be seen as miraculous? Perhaps when the odds against all the right conditions occurring at precisely the crucial moment are very high. Those who see a benign power at work throughout the natural world might claim that it was the intervention of Mother Nature, combined with the very best of modern medical knowledge and skill, that saved two-year-old Michael from almost certain death. Early on the morning of 19 January 1985, Michael woke up and wandered out into the garden of his parents' house in Milwaukee, Wisconsin, wearing only a light pair of pyjamas. The temperature had fallen to 60 degrees below zero. His father woke several hours later and, finding Michael missing, began to search frantically. At last he discovered his son's frozen body in the garden.

Michael's limbs were hardened. Ice crystals had formed on

and beneath his skin and he had stopped breathing. The body was taken to Milwaukee Children's Hospital where 18 doctors and 20 nurses worked on Michael for six hours. Dr Kevin Kelly, a specialist in hypothermia, described the infant as 'extremely dead'.

Doctors heard the ice crystals in his body cracking as they lifted Michael on to the operating table. As Michael's blood was warmed in a heart-lung machine and his body thawed, drugs were used to prevent his brain swelling. His arms and legs began swelling as fluid leaked from the ice-damaged cells, and incisions had to be made to allow the tissue to expand.

Dr Thomas Rice, who performed the operation, said that he knew of no one who had survived when the core of their body had dropped below –16°C, as Michael's had done. Michael remained semi-conscious for more than three days but afterwards made a rapid recovery.

There was minor muscle damage to his left hand and he has had some skin grafting on his limbs to cover the deep incisions. But Michael avoided brain damage because the wind-chill froze him so rapidly that his metabolism had very little need for oxygen.

The religious would say that God had answered the parents' prayers, the physicians that medical care had triumphed. It would be wrong and short-sighted to attribute miracles such as Michael's solely to divine intervention, for that would be to ignore hundreds of years of painstaking research. Equally blinkered is to see only the hand of man. Can miracles not be a partnership of human skill and divine or benign energies from beyond? Prayer, faith and medicine could, and certainly should, go hand in hand. That, to me, would seem the best conclusion.

Miraculous cures and recoveries, the sudden granting of fertility – these are all situations where the misfortunes we experience through chance or fate can suddenly be reversed, making the world seem a kinder, more just place. In the next chapter we continue this consideration of how miracles, or signs of blessing, can reveal order and meaning in an apparently random universe.

6

Signs of Blessing

Miraculous signs, where natural phenomena produce wondrous effects at sites of religious power, have been recorded from earliest times. Such indications of the blessing of a divine power have encouraged those of strong faith, and of none, that they are chosen and protected. Other sacred signs appear to individuals at home. They are seen only by the person involved and perhaps never shared except with those closest to them.

The dancing sun

Many cultures have considered the sun a symbol of divinity, from Ra in Ancient Egypt to Apollo in the Classical world. In more recent times, the sun has been observed dancing or spinning in holy places such as Fatima in Portugal and Medjugorje in the former Yugoslavia. Ann and Ken, who live in Crawley, Sussex, described how they saw the sun dancing in rural England. Their account is reconstructed from notes Ken took at the time:

> It was 4 August 1988. The soft green lawns of a stately home beside a ruined abbey, a cloudless sky and well over a thousand people were gathered for an open-air Mass celebrated by Bishop Taylor and 30 priests. We

were at the tiny Norfolk village of Walsingham, enjoying a five day pilgrimage entitled 'New Dawn in the Church'. We had gathered from all over the world – Brazil, Canada, the United States, Nigeria, Kenya, the Philippines, Poland, Portugal, Malta, France, Bosnia, Ireland and the United Kingdom. We were mainly Catholics, but there was a fair sprinkling of Orthodox and Protestant Christians. It was our last day of prayer, healing, talks, workshops, praise and worship.

We were standing on holy ground. In 1061, the local Lady of the Manor, Richeldie de Faverches, experienced a vision of the Blessed Virgin Mary. She was shown the house at Nazareth where Jesus lived and was requested to build a replica of it. This she did and for over 500 years Walsingham was known as a place of pilgrimage and healing. A great abbey was founded to care for the crowds of pilgrims and it lasted until Henry VIII's dissolution of the monasteries.

As we stood and knelt on the newly mown grass, there was an air of expectancy. The music group led us in praise. Faces were raised heavenwards, some with hope, some with pain, some in near ecstasy because of the nearness of God in this place. Perhaps it was because of the holy ground, perhaps the prayer and healing we received over the four days of the pilgrimage. After the Mass, we dispersed quietly and walked the mile or so back to our pilgrimage centre at the Slipper Chapel outside Walsingham.

That evening we gathered in the great marquee for a home-produced concert. We settled into our chairs and relaxed as, first the children's groups performed their acts, then a priest with a guitar, then a group from the Philippines.

Suddenly it happened. In the middle of the next act, people started leaving the tent, a few at a time at first, then in groups, then dozens all around the marquee. The singers stopped and one of the singers announced into the microphone, 'I think they have seen something. Perhaps we had better join them.'

Then I heard someone close by exclaim, 'The sun is dancing!'

We emerged into the fresh air. Our group had to crawl under the tent flaps because all the entrances were now crowded with people leaving. Outside, in our corner of the field, 50 or so people were gazing up into the sky, some praying, some weeping, some transfixed by what they could see. I looked up – how can I ever explain the inexplicable, describe the indescribable or even begin to relate the wonder of what was happening in the sky?

The evening sun had apparently done the impossible. It had come closer to the earth and was actually in front of a small cloud in the otherwise clear sky. The sun was immediately behind a large grey disc, like a communion host, so that only the outer rim of its light might be seen. Both sun and disc were dancing together, spinning and vibrating with wonderfully beautiful colours shooting out all around them.

I stared at it for half an hour or more until it set in the usual way, still dancing. I was on my knees, most of us were. I could only think, 'Why are we so privileged to witness this? Why me?'

We were all standing or kneeling in sheer wonder, some of us weeping quietly with joy. Isabelle, who comes from Crawley also, asked me if I was all right and I replied, 'No, I shall never be the same again.'

This is true. How could I ever be the same after this? It was so beautiful and wonderful, it was almost like seeing God face to face and living to tell the tale. We discovered later most of us saw slightly different colours and manifestations and some saw nothing at all, only the evening sun setting as it always does, too bright to gaze on for more than a second. Why were we blessed, why were we chosen? I felt and still feel completely humbled.

I wrote down the details the same evening. I cannot offer any explanation within the bounds of present scientific knowledge. The dancing sun was seen by thousands at Fatima in 1917 and has been witnessed hundreds of times by the crowds of pilgrims who go to

Medjugorje in Bosnia. Now it occurred in England at the shrine of Walsingham. What does it mean?

My own assessment is that we are in an age of signs and wonders – all come with one simple message for the world, repent, pray, turn back to God and work for peace and unity among the different churches and between Christians and other believers. Medjugorje is a case in point. It is an oasis of peace in war-torn Bosnia. Only two shells have fallen on the village and it has brought together Catholics, Orthodox Christians and Muslims in peace and harmony.

The effects of the dancing sun on my own faith are more certain because I can never deny what I saw, what I know and perhaps I can never entirely lose my faith now. At times when I feel down or am lacking faith, I remember Walsingham and say to myself with relief and joy, 'It's true, it's all true.'

I know now exactly what Jesus means when he says so often, 'Your reward in heaven will be great' because I have been privileged to have been given just a tiny sample of that reward, have had just a brief glimpse of the heavenly glory.

One of the most noteworthy aspects of this incident is that some people seeing the sun dance at Walsingham experienced different visions, varying colours and manifestations, while some saw nothing. This suggests that there are no objective criteria by which such moments of wonder can be measured. Mary from County Wicklow in Ireland, whose account appeared in Chapter 1, not only saw her statue of the Virgin Mary weep, but witnessed the figure moving and opening and closing her eyes. Those that try to measure or analyse the tears alone in such a manifestation may prove that the liquid was resin, red ochre or some other substance involved in the original manufacture. However that is only one aspect of what may be a total transformative experience, triggered perhaps by an explicable physical phenomenon but leading to a real spiritual awakening and to cures from life-threatening illnesses.

Where fraud has been proven, as in some cases in Europe,

the owners' main concern may have been to prove to a disbelieving world that what they originally saw was a genuine experience. Demanding scientific verification of a spiritual experience can ironically lead to the kind of falsification that destroys the original essence. It also denies those who wish to study such phenomena a chance to approach the heart rather than the mechanics of the miracle.

~ *Religious visions* ~

Glenys, unlike Ken, was alone when she saw a flaming cross when she was just 14 and the experience has over the years remained a private one:

> I am not sure whether I had gone to sleep and woken up or had not yet gone to sleep. I looked up at the crucifix which hung above the bed and there were flames leaping from it. I was quite scared and put my head under the sheets, supposing it would not be there when I looked again. However, when I did look, the flames were still shooting from it.
>
> I watched the fiery cross for some time. I did not attempt to tell my mother. Indeed, I did not tell anyone at the time for I did not think they would believe me. I eventually got under the bedclothes and went back to sleep. I have always been quite religious, but have lived a very ordinary life and nothing similar has ever happened since.

Glenys's experience had the immediate result of making her less afraid of the dark. On a deeper level it was a confirmation of her religious faith. But these signs do not have to be of religious significance to be wonderful and special to those witnessing them. Although the secular miracle has not been studied in any depth, it is often only the context within which the experience is interpreted that makes it differ from religious experiences.

Robert's family were members of the Church of England when he had his experience. Yet now, many years later, he does not interpret what he saw as a sign that he was chosen by God. Often adults looking back on childhood experiences come to appreciate that they were not, as adults told them at the time, just a result of childish imagination, but actually reflected a child's natural ability to tap other dimensions.

Robert recalls that, when he was six or seven, he and his brother Jack saw in the sky very distinctly a fiery chariot with a cloaked driver, pulled by six fiery horses:

> The whole thing moved across the sky, turned and came back. The horses were galloping quite naturally. I ran downstairs to tell my mother. She paid no attention to me. I forget what happened next. Presumably I went back to look. Jack tells me that while I was away he saw a fiery cross in the sky. I have a vague mental picture of that, but I cannot be certain that I saw the cross. I cannot explain the phenomenon, but I am sure it happened.
>
> I have never been tempted to regard myself as privileged because of what I saw. I would not say the experience was religious but preternatural. I believe children can see what is denied to those who have reached the age of reason. I felt childish excitement at the time. I see the experience as evidence of another form of existence, though I am not convinced it was religious as such.

One pre-Christian interpretation of Robert's experience would be that he saw the Norse 'Wild Hunt'. There have been reports through the ages, and from across Europe, of 'ghost riders in the sky': mounted huntsmen, sometimes with dogs, representatives of Odin, chasing their prey across the heavens.

However, the strangest vision of which I have heard was one that occurred near Bombay during the Second World War, which could have come straight from the pages of Milton's *Paradise Lost*. Richard, who in Chapter 3 described an escape from almost certain death in South Africa while serving in the navy, recalled:

I was on the MV *Potaru* bound for Singapore with a cargo of ammunition. En route, we were diverted to Bombay. We were only a few days' sailing from Bombay and I was standing on the stern with three or four crew members. The sky was blue and cloudless. After a while a few wisps of white cloud appeared and joined together into a single cloud just above our port quarter.

Before those wisps joined together they were white. Almost as soon as they formed a single cloud, it became dark grey in some parts and in others black. Then it turned with a perfect face of Lucifer. There were no fuzzy outlines at all. It was as though the face had been etched into the sky. There he was smiling down on us.

His hair was black and slicked back with a centre parting. His ears were long and pointed at the top. Lucifer had a Van Dyck beard and his lips were parted in a smile. His cheeks were dimpled. We could even see the white of his eyes and his pupils.

I felt very uneasy looking at Satan and I know the others did, although none of us spoke. How long we stood there gazing up at him I don't know. The silence was broken by a deckhand who said, 'I'm going for my camera to get a picture of him.' But, as soon as he returned, the cloud broke up before he could focus his camera.

If there was a hidden portent in this I do not know. I myself was put ashore in Bombay and joined the *Ascanius*. The strange thing was that none of the men who saw Lucifer spoke about it to the others but I am sure they felt just as spooked as I did. I often wondered if it was a portent of things to come but, if so, for whom was it intended?

Clouds have been used for scrying since ancient times. Scrying is a method of seeing pictures, whether in a crystal, a candle flame or in natural sources, such as the embers of a fire or patterns made by ripples in water. By their shapes such signs were taken as a sign of blessing or warning. Perhaps Richard saw the evil of war personified. It is no less credible than those who see angels and yet visions of evil are often not reported for fear perhaps of being seen as tainted by the evil.

If one follows the Eastern idea that there must be evil as well as good, darkness as well as light, then Richard's experience is equally wondrous, though more chilling to behold.

Unlike the sailors, Ivy managed to capture a far more benign cloud vision than Richard's on camera, which years later has formed the focus for a shrine of healing. Ivy was taking a picture of a rainbow over her home near Woombye, South-East Queensland, in early 1980. However, it was not until some time after the film had been developed that she saw in the photograph the image of the Madonna and Child in the cloud. Ivy herself was a non-Catholic but the local Catholic community became very excited by the picture. There seems to be no physical explanation for the image, such as double exposure, and Ivy possessed no icons that could have appeared in the picture by mistake. The photograph was taken outside the window and the sun was behind Ivy as she took the picture. The mystery remains.

What is even more remarkable is that, ten years later, a Croatian-Australian mystic, Susanna D'Amore, bought some land close to Ivy's former property and built a chapel, after she herself had seen a vision of the Virgin Mary near the spot where the picture had been taken. Susanna also discovered a spring with healing properties close by. Now pilgrims come from miles away on the thirteenth day of the month and priests celebrate Mass in the chapel. Witnesses have claimed to see the sun dance over the chapel, another sign of the presence of the Virgin Mary.

~ *Permanent transformations* ~

Like Ivy's photograph, miraculous signs may be etched on the physical world. However, sacred objects can also undergo permanent physical changes that assure those who experience the phenomena that they are blessed. Des, who lives in Bristol, visited Medjugorje in February 1991 with his wife Charmaine. He told me:

> Not long before I went to Medjugorje, I had started to use my rosary after quite a lapse in time because of

family troubles. As a result, I believe my prayers were answered. My rosary was very special to me as it had been given to me in 1979 by my mother when I still lived in Ireland. It was made up of brown wooden beads, linked by small steel-coloured chains.

We went to Mass on our first day in Medjugorje and during the service I took my rosary from my pocket and saw a thread of gold running through it. I turned to Charmaine and showed her and her eyes lit with joy. Then the transformation stopped but the links that had changed colour remained a brassy gold.

The strange thing was that not all the links had changed colour, but those that had were in a definite pattern. The four sets of chains running from the cross to the centre were now gold and at ten regular intervals along the rosary the links had also changed to gold.

At first, I was quite upset. I had heard of the phenomena of links on rosaries changing to gold at Medjugorje but I had not expected it would happen to me. I was suddenly confronted by evidence of another reality. Before that I had hoped that God was true. Now I was shocked to discover that He was indeed true and that I, an ordinary man, had received personal Grace from our Lady.

I asked myself why 14 sections of the rosary had changed and not all the rest. Had all the links changed colour, I might have been persuaded that they had been like that all the time or that it was a chemical change because of something in the atmosphere. But the pattern was so definite. Then I realised it was the fourteenth day of the month.

The same day I climbed the mountain and for the first time in 25 years followed the Stations of the Cross. There were 14 and now I understood that 14 changes referred to the difficult road I had to travel.

The experience has altered me on a deep level. When I came back to England, I really believed and gave voice to my faith more openly to other people where before I would have held back. My rosary is very precious to me now and my prayers are not just words but heartfelt.

> Most of all I have a tremendous sense of peace and certainty that I will be protected.

In the first chapter, I described how Dennis's rosary changed colour as he sat by his wife's bedside. He, too, saw it as a sign of grace and Christine recovered against all medical prognoses. Both experiences had a religious background, the bedside of a comatose woman where her husband sat in prayer and a holy shrine. But Adrian's experience occurred in the wilderness in Australia at a time when religion was far from his mind. Adrian, who is 62, was walking along a private road on his wheat farm near Beverley, about 100 miles from Perth. It was in December 1995 and Adrian's 30-year-old son was with him. Suddenly Adrian heard a voice coming from a pile of rocks, telling him that the Lord would show him the way. His son did not hear the voice, but the next night they returned to see a shaft of moonlight illuminating the rock.

As they walked over to it, the face of Christ appeared in the rock. Adrian was only an occasional churchgoer but is convinced that he witnessed a miracle that night.

Opinions among the 1,400 people living in Beverley are divided. Some think they have also beheld a miracle as they have seen the face in the rock. Others insist it is a hoax and a tourist trap. However, it is said that the face fulfils an Aboriginal elder's 15-year-old prediction that divinity would appear in the town. Other paranormal phenomena have also occurred in the area over a period of time, such as crop circles and mysterious lights in the sky over the town.

Local silk-screen printer Annie attempted to explain away the miracle when she discovered a stock reproduction of Christ that is universally regarded as bearing a striking resemblance to the 'Miracle Rock' while she scrolled through a computer art software package in search of a suitable graphic for T-shirts. But others, including Adrian, suggest that the computer graphic artist may have been divinely inspired and point out considerable differences in the features between the computer image and the face in the rock. Many depictions of Christ are similar – not surprisingly if they are to be likenesses.

In spite of scepticism, pilgrims have continued to visit the rock and have drawn great inspiration from it. Deanne, a local shopkeeper, commented: 'All those who have visited here from out of town have been lovely people who believed what they saw was real.'

A 93-year-old woman was driven for six hours to see the rock and many of the pilgrims were obviously not well-to-do people. Local professional psychic Roma Paton examined the energy fields of the miracle rock and asserts its authenticity. 'Its energy field is very different from granite. I sensed no density from the rock or the quarry around it,' she said. 'If it is a hoax, then that doesn't explain the strange light my husband and I saw over Beverley the night it was found or the crop rings which appeared three weeks earlier.'

Beverley Shire clerk Keith Beyers, who offered the use of the town hall free of charge for the rock's display, said: 'I just wish Adrian would get the rock examined scientifically – not for my own sake but so that he won't have to put up with the flak.'

Adrian replied that he has made an open, although conditional offer, to any experts who want to examine the rock but no one has approached him. Like many of those who own miraculous objects, he can see no point in trying to authenticate his find. 'How can you authenticate the handwriting of God?' he asks. 'I was fully expecting the backlash from the sceptics but the faith of so many well-wishers has been enough to keep me going.'

To the Aborigines, sacred images in rock are confirmation of what they know on the deepest level, that the earth is the living essence of the spirit and that only if we respect it can we live harmoniously on it. Perhaps Adrian's experience is such a reminder that the earth itself is sacred.

Evidence that such phenomena are possible comes from an American judge, used to sifting evidence dispassionately, who himself witnessed a similar, albeit momentary, physical manifestation. In September, Judge Leslie Isaiah Gaines was climbing the steps of Hamilton County Courthouse when he saw the face of Christ on one of the marble pillars. The Judge, who described his experience as 'a wake-up call from God', saw great sorrow in Jesus's expression. The face was bearded, with bloodstained eyes, and was crowned with thorns.

It was not until the following March that Judge Gaines sent a fax, telling reporters of the vision that he said had given him daily inspiration ever since. He unknowingly sent the fax on the 110th anniversary of the death of Captain John Desmond who had died defending the courthouse from a lynch mob. His statue stands in the lobby of the courthouse. The face of Jesus, as described by the Judge, resembled that of the martyred Ohio guardsman.

~ *Multi-faith miracles* ~

Miraculous signs are found in all faiths and, in increasingly multicultural societies, are seen as signs of blessing on the whole community. Indeed, all who came to see the Muslim sign of grace in March 1996, in a terraced home in Bolton, Lancashire, were made welcome. Salim, a local mill worker, opened his house to pilgrims from all over Britain who came to view the open aubergine, fruit of the egg plant, which spelled out in its dark seeds the message in Arabic script *Ya Allah*, 'Allah exists' or by another translation 'Oh Allah'.

Salim's wife Ruksana, a mother of two, told reporters that she had had a predictive dream:

> I bought three aubergines from the local shop and the same night I had a dream telling me that one of the aubergines was holy. When I opened it, I would find Allah.
>
> When I got up, I discovered my dream was true. As I cut one of the aubergines open, the seeds spelled out the name of our God. Although I have always been religious, now I believe with all my heart.

After Ruksana discovered the message, Salim ran to tell the local priest who confirmed it as a miracle. Salim began leaving his front door open because about 50 people a day come to see what Muslims believe is a wondrous sign of grace. Abdullah Patel, the priest of the local Masjide-Gosia

Mosque, commented that the sign was wonderful for Salim and the community as a whole, 'because things like this happen only to good people and are a sign of blessing upon the community. It reveals the truth to non-believers.'

Salim planned to leave the aubergine on display in the mosque for a few weeks and then share out small pieces to the faithful to be eaten raw.

In 1990, 4,500 pilgrims came to marvel at a similarly marked aubergine at the home of Zahid in Leicester. Other aubergine fruits, bearing the name of Allah in their seeds, were discovered in Birmingham, Nottingham and Burton-on-Trent, all Midland industrial towns. More than a thousand visitors saw the holy aubergine belonging to Hussein, an accountant who lives in Nottingham. His son preserved the aubergine in saline solution.

Hussein commented on those who suggested the miracle was 'man-made': 'A man cannot write inside an aubergine. If you cut it open and try, you will be left with big holes on one side. It is done with instructions from Allah. His angels are at work.'

The most widespread sign of divine blessing that has occurred in modern times must be the 'milk miracle', briefly mentioned in Chapter 1. This miracle was witnessed on Thursday, 21 September 1995, all over the world. Milk is the sacred fluid of Hindus, regarded in much the same way as holy water in Christianity. The ritual offering of milk, fruit, sweets and money to the gods is an established practice and milk is poured over Shiva and Ganesh, his son, during festivals. The milk miracle was apparently foretold in the Punjab. Pandit Chaman Prakash, head of the Khampur Shiv Mandir Temple in Chandigargh, was approached by a young woman before sunrise on Thursday who told him that her sister had dreamed that Ganesh would come to earth to drink milk at 4am. The priest reluctantly opened the temple but at 4am, as predicted, the statue accepted milk from a spoon.

News spread through India and to communities all around the world. In India, statues of Ganesh were reported to be drinking milk on Thursday morning. Within hours, millions of Hindus all over the world flocked to their nearest temple.

By Thursday evening the phenomenon was being reported in Calcutta, Madras, Singapore, Hong Kong, Indonesia, Bangladesh, Nepal, Dubai, Kenya, Germany, Bangkok, Brisbane, Toronto, New York, Jersey City and throughout Britain. Other idols, Shiva, Krishna and Brahma, were also accepting milk.

The phenomenon was popularly seen as a sign that the problems of the world would be overcome. Britain's one million Hindus, who retain close links with their families in India, were quickly swept along in the general excitement. Much of the activity centred on the temple in Southall.

Explaining why she had come with thousands of others to the temple in suburban West London, Madhu, who is 40, said: 'My mother called from Punjab and said practically the whole of India had come to a standstill. My sister called to tell me her own brass deity was taking milk, so I had to come and try for myself. And it is true.'

From India, where believers say the phenomenon marks either an important birth or signifies a message from God, confirmation came by Friday afternoon that Ganesh and the other deities had ceased drinking.

'The gods are now satiated and will not accept any more milk,' said Baburam Gosai, a priest at the Kalibari temple in Delhi.

In Britain, secular Hindu professionals struggled to explain away a phenomenon that many of them experienced personally. Jitesh Thakrar, a solicitor, admitted that milk was accepted from his spoon when he visited the Southall Temple on Thursday night. 'It happened also to an English vicar,' he said. 'I have no explanation but this will give Hindus a greater sense of confidence.'

What is more, Rikee Verma reported in *The Times* newspaper that he had gone to his household altar and placed a spoonful of milk against a photograph of Ganesh. Half a teaspoon had disappeared within seconds and yet the glass was dry. Some of Britain's leading Indian intellectuals attempted to analyse the long-term consequences of the event on the Hindu population.

Bhikhu Parekh, Professor of Political Theory at Hull

University, who was born a Hindu but is now an agnostic, remarked:

> I don't believe in miracles. The explanation is not perhaps hysteria but what psychologists call suggestion. But why do people believe in miracles, not the physics but the sociology? In Christian society, when people are confused they look for a second coming. Hindus don't take that view of history.

His view is: 'There is a Hindu feeling of self-confidence – politically, culturally and economically. God is smiling on them, saying, "You are on the right lines. I am with you".'

A consultant psychiatrist, Dr Raj Persaud, another Hindu who is now also an agnostic, said he, too, did not believe in miracles, certainly not mundane ones such as idols sipping milk. 'The real point is not whether miracles are occurring. It's that the event has shown the power of religion.'

He added: 'As psychiatrists we give people drugs and medicine but we tend to ignore the ability of religion to comfort people. There is a strong link between suffering and faith. Religion helps us to cope with suffering.'

The fundamentalist World Hindu Council, Vishwa Hindu Parishad, declared the milk-drinking a divine event, a miracle. Scientists, however, declared the milk was absorbed by capillary action through the pores and cracks of the statues.

Although by the Sunday the milk miracle had entirely ceased with Hindu deities, there were reports of the phenomenon beyond that faith. Karen, who is 31 and lives in Runcorn in Cheshire, said that her 4-foot statute of the Virgin Mary accepted nine spoonfuls of milk. Later the same day, another Blessed Virgin statue was accepting milk in Kuala Lumpar in Malaysia.

Scientists have put forward many theories to explain away the milk miracle, such as capillary action and natural absorption by marble. But the fact is that the statues did not before and have not since accepted milk. What is more, where statues were tiny or made of solid metal as many were, there seems no adequate explanation. The problem is that, in demanding proof or seeking evidence of fraudulence, sometimes the sheer wonder of such happenings can be lost.

Peggy Mason, a respected Western expert on religious phenomena, discounts the explanations of scientists and psychiatrists on the milk-drinking idols:

> The idols drank the milk offered to them for one day only in September 1995 throughout the world. The phenomenon occurred not only in public places of worship but private homes. Milk offered to Ganesh in a temple in Wimbledon also disappeared while simultaneously in a shrine room with a large photograph of Sai Baba, *vibhuti* [fragrant sacred healing ash] poured from Baba's forehead and nectar poured from his feet. For scientists to say that stone can become porous is ridiculous, since the phenomena occurred only in one day and simultaneously throughout the world.

Chapter 10 describes some of the miracles performed by Sai Baba, who is regarded by his devotees as God incarnate.

~ *Miracles of nature* ~

Miraculous signs are often dismissed precisely because they have a physical explanation. Yet a continuing physical wonder can form a focus for smaller personal transformations and healing. On 16 and 17 April 1995, 300,000 people gathered on a South Korean beach to celebrate the miracle of the sea parting. Every year for an hour on two consecutive days, a powerful tide divides the water between Jindo and Modo Islands to reveal a 1.7 mile path between the two islands. This event has gained profound religious significance, perhaps because it does reveal the wondrous aspects of nature, and thousands of pilgrims walk the path between the waters.

The annual 'miracle' is traditionally attributed to Grandma Mulberry, who lived on Jindo 500 years ago. Today her small shrine on the beach holds a painting of her in white robes. Local women light incense at the shrine and pray for her help.

Local holy men perform rituals for good harvests and to overcome the spirits of evil.

Legend has it that Grandmother Mulberry lived in a mountain village that was threatened by tigers. The villagers sailed off to Modo on a raft but Grandma Mulberry was left behind.

The old lady entreated the Dragon Lord to allow her to cross the water to Modo and it is said that the seas parted and the path was sent to take her to safety. A less spiritually satisfying version suggests she was unable to reach the other side before the waters joined once more and that she drowned.

However it is believed that from that time the natural phenomenon has occurred annually as a sign of divine favour. Whether Grandmother Mulberry is a symbol or an actuality, the annual parting of the sea is a reminder of the wonders of the natural world that in themselves remind us of the infinite power of the universe.

I asked Rabbi Dr Julian Jacobs, Minister of Ealing Synagogue and a leading theologian, about miracles. Rabbi Dr Jacobs replied:

> Since God is all-powerful there is in principle no reason why He cannot perform miracles. There may well be things in life and nature that cannot be explained in any other way.
>
> In practice, however, God usually chooses to act only through natural means and events. One cannot therefore prove that a miracle has taken place. A miracle lies in the eyes of the beholder and in his understanding of the conjunction of events or other circumstances. There is in Judaism no question of verification of a miracle by an established body.
>
> Many would regard the wonders of nature, day and night, the rising of the sun, the change of seasons, childbirth, life itself as miracles. It is a mistake to look for miracles only in dramatic one-time occurrences. Man is surrounded by unrecognised miraculous events.
>
> Judaism plays down the importance of miracles. Irrespective of miracles, truly religious people believe in God because they have faith.

At the other end of the spectrum, nature can offer a personal sign of blessing. David's son Simon died of leukaemia when he was only 11 years old. While Simon was ill, David and his wife, who are scientists, used to take their son out in their boat and would often anchor just off Studland Bay in Dorset, one of Simon's favourite spots. When he was younger, Simon was always concerned about a group of rocks at the entrance to the bay that would appear at low water, fearing that the boat might hit them.

After Simon's funeral, David and his wife, Alison, took the ashes out in the boat at the weekend to Studland Bay to bury them but could not find a place that was right. David told me they went to sleep in a troubled state of mind, but when they woke next morning they saw Blind Rock sticking out of the water at low tide. They knew instinctively that this was the place to bury their son's ashes and decided to return each year on the anniversary to plant flowers on the rock in Simon's memory.

Two years later, David and Alison had to go to Florida on business on the anniversary day and, since their flight left England at 10.30 am, they were unable to visit Studland Bay. The weather was bad and the visibility poor and they felt very sad, as the plane began its ascent, that they were unable to be at Studland with Simon. Suddenly, there was a break in the clouds and brilliant sunlight. The Isle of Wight could be seen quite clearly and minutes later the plane flew over Studland Bay which could also be clearly seen. David says that it was more than coincidence that the sun should break through at that precise moment and he felt they had been able to fulfil their promise to Simon and be close to him.

Was this a case of synchronicity, one of the meaningful coincidences recognised by Jung at the heart of much psychic phenomena or was it a sign from Simon that he was with them? The break in the bad weather lasted only those few vital seconds as the plane flew over Studland Bay. The routes taken by planes can vary by many miles but on that day sun and air conditions conspired to enable a grieving couple to fulfil their promise. David told me he has since had many such signs that convince both him and Alison that Simon is still with them in essence and they work tirelessly to find a cure for the disease that killed him.

The Reverend Tom Willis believes that a miracle, whether it is the majestic parting of the Red Sea or the simple comfort derived by Simon's parents that their son was not lost, is no less wondrous for being rooted in natural energies.

The next chapter looks at some of the 'simple miracles' that individuals have experienced in their daily lives. It does not always take a life-and-death situation for a miracle to occur. Sometimes a person with a very ordinary problem seems to receive an extremely practical helping hand from above.

7

Everyday Miracles

'What is a miracle?' I asked in the Introduction to this book. It is not so difficult to define an escape from death, a dramatic spontaneous recovery from a potentially fatal disease, a spinning sun or a statue that drinks milk as miraculous. But the majority of people who speak of miracles in their own lives, or those of their close relatives, experience events that may appear less spectacular but have just as much significance to them. Miracles that are small in the world's terms but vital on a personal level give us a sense that we are protected and that a miracle does not have to qualify for a place on a television documentary to have a profound effect. Minor miracles begin in people's everyday lives and often bring practical positive results in answer to a prayer spoken or unspoken.

Signs that God cares for us all

The Reverend Tom Willis believes firmly in small miracles as a guiding force in his own life and proof that God really does care enough to answer our daily needs, as well as move mountains and part the oceans. At the time we spoke, I was not entirely convinced that any deity could really concern himself with the minutiae of the universe, but Tom described the miracles in his own life with great conviction:

In religious miracles God acts in answer to a prayer or cry for help. Sometimes it is possible to work out in physical terms how a miracle happens but it is the timing that makes the event miraculous. Such miracles may not be life-and-death issues but be of vital importance to the person concerned. I have experienced many small miracles in my own life, in response to prayer, and they are equally a sign that God cares for every one of us.

For example, at one time a friend, Emma, was living with us with her children, as she had lost her husband and needed a new home. My wife and I had been out for lunch and on the way back passed a house that was for sale privately, which we knew would be just perfect for Emma.

We went home and my wife said that Emma and I had just enough time to go and see the house before tea as it was quite a few miles away, near Hull. The people were at home, allowed us to look round and, sure enough, Emma did like the house. However, she hesitated about making an offer there and then, although it was a time when good houses were going like hot cakes and prices were rising daily.

By the time we got home Emma had decided to make an offer on the house after all and wanted to do so at once, before anyone else did and the price was raised. But Emma had forgotten the name of the people selling the house. So I asked God to help me find the telephone number so we could reserve the house straight away. Emma really needed that house and it was a price she could afford.

The phone book for the Hull area had about 100,000 names in it. It fell open at H and for some reason my hand went straight down the middle column to Harrison, although it was not a name I recalled. Then I understood. There at the top of the page was the address of the people next door to the house Emma wanted. I rang through to ask for the phone number of their next-door neighbours, who were not on the phone. But the Harrisons promised to go next door and tell them Emma wanted the house and to leave our phone number which Emma had not done.

I believe that you can pray for anything if it is a right purpose. Sceptics ask how God can possibly attend to the needs of everyone who calls Him. Even a computer can cope with hundreds of thousands of messages coming into it and that is made by humans. I have five children and I can attend to all their needs and be aware that they are all different. If God created the universe, as I believe, then He can love us all and acknowledge our needs, great and small. I am always amazed by the intricacy of God's love for us all in every aspect of our lives.

People say that such happenings are coincidences but we cannot rely on coincidences, whereas we can rely on asking God. Sometimes He will say no and later we see why. God will answer our prayers if something is right for us and will not harm ourselves or others. If we prayed for a million pounds for ourselves we probably would not get it because that would not be good for us. But it is possible for money to be given seemingly out of the blue for good causes.

Another time I desperately needed a new suit. I had been asked to become President of the local Mentally Handicapped Society, as I have a mentally handicapped son and there had been a lot of friction in the club. It was felt I could heal the breach and so I agreed. My first duty was to attend a big charity event at the town hall and accept a cheque from the Lord Mayor on behalf of the Society.

I do not worry at all about clothes, but I felt it was my duty to look my best for the Society. My old black suit was shabby and worn at the cuffs. I was totally broke at the time and so I prayed for just enough money to buy a suit so that I would not let the Society down.

Every morning I went to the door to fetch the post in case there was a tax rebate or some unexpected cheque. But there was nothing and, as the days ticked by, I wondered if it was God's will that I was humbled and went in my old suit. I even wondered about blacking the cuffs and hoped it would not come off during the evening. Three or four days before the event, I realised it was too late even if money did arrive. Because of my build, I am not a stock size and I need to have suits specially made. There simply would not be time.

Then, on the day I had to attend the presentation, I found a huge black bin bag of clothes at my front door. This was quite common, as people used to leave their old cast-offs and jumble for me to give to 'down and outs' and meths drinkers. For the first time ever, I tipped the bag out on the floor and there was a practically brand-new dark charcoal grey/black suit. I tried it on and it fitted me like a glove. 'Thank you, God,' I said.

I later made tactful enquiries as to the origin of the bag and discovered the people concerned had been reluctant to put the suit in with the jumble. It seemed a waste because clothes were usually ruined within a few days by the recipients. I think the suit had not been worn because of a bereavement. The family were so pleased it had been used to such good effect and I wore my 'miracle suit', as the family called it, until it wore out.

If we ask and if it is right, our prayers are answered in ways that can only be described as miraculous. The small miracle is as precious as the large for it assures us of God's daily love.

Tom's view of the universe is immensely reassuring. He is not a man who lives in an ivory tower, but has been out on the front-line fighting evil. He has also known great sorrow in his own life. Tom's own son was born with Down's Syndrome many years ago. He felt impelled to go to the church to give thanks, although he could not understand why. Many people asked him how God could give his own vicar a handicapped child. Tom pointed out that to cast such sorrows only on non-believers would conflict with the idea of a loving God and that loving God does not give you immunity from the world's sorrows. However, he believes that his son has bought immense happiness to others and wisdom and compassion to the family.

When I talk to sceptics with frowning faces who tell me there is nothing but dust and ashes ahead and that belief in anything apart from the material world is delusion, and I then listen to Tom, I know whom I would prefer to take me over at the Final Trumpet.

Daniel, who lives in Northumberland, is a Catholic. Like Tom, he accepts that God is active in our lives on a mundane level:

> On one occasion, when I was still living at my parents' home in South London, I needed to be up at 5.30 am for an interview some distance from home. I did not have an alarm. When I went to bed the night before the interview, I prayed that I would awake at 5.30 am. Like most people, in such circumstances, when I am anxious not to oversleep, I normally have a broken night, waking frequently to check my watch. On this occasion, however, I had an unbroken night of perfect sleep and, at 5.30 in the morning, my crucifix fell to the floor with a bang and woke me. It had been above my bed for several years and had never fallen before. I do not know whether the nail on which it hung had gradually become insecure, but even if this were so, the timing of the crucifix's fall was remarkable.

~ *Gifts from God* ~

Few miracles, are, as this book shows, guarantees of a life of ease and everlasting joy. Daniel has had many sorrows in his life. Many of those touched by a wondrous event great or small say that, in times of trouble, they try to hold on to the brief assurance of grace the experience offered. By their nature, most miracles are performed in times of crisis and sorrow and those who know little of suffering rarely experience such moments of wonder.

One of the most frightening situations is to be homeless with a small child and no money. It seems as though only a miracle or an angel can help. I have myself been alone with two small children in a tumbledown cottage with moneylenders banging at the door. I was rescued by my second husband. Angels take many forms but few, like Janet's, come in the guise of a bank manager. Janet is now in her seventies and lives near Brighton. She described her escape from abject poverty and homelessness:

> My husband had many affairs and slowly but surely they destroyed me. We were on our way to the Midlands, once again a move away from an affair, and we passed along a road through a steep bank covered in bluebells. I suddenly knew, as I looked at the mass of blue, that area would change my life in a significant way. I felt cold and afraid but I knew there was no going back.
>
> In spite of promises that my husband really had changed, the old pattern continued, another affair following soon after our arrival in the new town. This time my husband told me that he was moving the woman and her children into my home and I would have to share my son's bedroom in future. The woman lived close to the bluebell wood. When I protested my husband insisted that he would make me accept the situation or I could get out and that the fault was mine for having Victorian values. My heart broke then. I went to the kitchen and cried, 'Dear God tell me, what can I do, where can I go?'
>
> As I stood sobbing I felt my late father's hand on my shoulder and he spoke to me. 'You must divorce him, my girl.'
>
> I caught a bus into the city centre – I did not know what to do but I could not stay in that house. The bus made a detour and I found myself getting off the bus right outside a solicitor's office. I went in and said I wanted a divorce.
>
> After the divorce, I was left at 46 years old with nothing, no money, no home, only a single ticket on a coach southwards for myself and my son. We arrived at High Wycombe station and had to wait some minutes while a long goods train passed through. As I sat waiting, I noticed on top of a hill a lovely large golden dome with

a cross on top. A voice said quite clearly, 'Name your new bungalow Golden Cross.'

It was ludicrous. My son and I were homeless, hungry and cold. We were reduced to huddling in launderettes to keep warm. I was as low as any person can get. At our destination, I pushed my courage to the limit, walked into a bank and asked to see the manager. To my surprise, the manager saw me there and then and I told him that I needed money to buy a home to give my son a sense of security and new roots. The bank manager looked at me in amazement. 'What collateral can you offer?' he asked.

'Nothing but these,' I said, holding up my hands, palms facing him.

'I will let you know,' he replied. I turned away. It was hopeless. I did not even have a job or a permanent address. He took my name and the address of the bed and breakfast where we were staying and I hit despair full in the face.

The next day a message came for me to call into the bank. I was given a mortgage and over the following years paid it back, every penny, by taking any work I could, all the work I could. When I was ill and could not work, the bank manager asked me how I could pay the arrears. I said I did not know but I would pay as I had before and I did. I bought a bungalow and named it 'Golden Cross' and it gave my son security and roots.

Many, many years later, I met the manager and asked why he had given me a mortgage against all reason. Had I defaulted he would have been in serious trouble – how he managed to arrange the mortgage I will never know.

He replied, 'You held up your hands to me. I knew I had to help you, whatever the cost, and I knew you would not let me down.'

I have been through the depths of despair but when you are at the bottom of a pit the only way to go is upwards. These experiences have made me very wise, very confident and taught me to live life to the full.

Janet worked to fulfil the bank manager's faith in her. In so many miracles, the unexpected help, the moment of illumination, must be followed by years of effort, whether in working to pay a mortgage while bringing up a child alone or facing years of surgery as Fiona in Chapter 2 did, after she was saved from death beneath the blades of a speedboat. A miracle frequently acts as a catalyst for human endeavour.

According to philosophies such as Quakerism, there would be sufficient in the world to feed and clothe mankind if everyone handed on the money or goods they did not require to those in more need. Unfortunately, most of the time, the world does not work on this principle. So when such a helping hand arrives quite naturally, at exactly the right time, it seems nothing less than miraculous. Sheila, who is Jewish, lives in Los Angeles. I met her on a US television programme, *The Other Side*, and we became penfriends. She wrote to me of her own small miracle:

> In 1977, after I divorced my husband, I was left with a car that always seemed to be in the garage. Aside from working to put food on the table, most of my money seemed to go on repairs on my car. I would go to the movies and see cars being demolished and I would cry.
>
> How, when I needed a car so desperately, could the movie industry so flamboyantly drive cars off cliffs and blow them up? One day a client of my boss stopped at my desk and invited me to lunch. We went to what was then the very elegant Beverly Wilshire Hotel to lunch. He suggested he was interested in me and wanted to buy me an outfit he saw on one of the models in the fashion show. I ignored the suggestion and thought that was the end of things.
>
> The following weekend he called me at home on Sunday and said that he and his wife were going on a cruise and he would like to book a passage for me. I laughed and I told him that even if I wanted to go, I did not have a proper wardrobe. He told me that he would provide that for me as well. The phone call had woken me up and I don't think I was fully absorbing everything he was saying.

I laughed again and told him, as I looked at my closet, I had enough clothes and I did not need a cruise. He asked me what I did need and I told him that I needed, more than anything, a car that worked. He told me to meet him at his bank the following day, Monday, at noon. I could not believe what was going on and after we said our goodbyes I went back to sleep and when I awoke the second time, I thought that what I remembered was a lovely dream. I put it out of my mind.

The following morning my new acquaintance phoned me early to remind me that I needed to meet him at his bank at noon. I did and he handed me a cashier's cheque for $5000. I was able to purchase a good used car which lasted me for the next five years. He called me several times over the years to see how I was, but we never had a relationship nor were any demands to have one made on me. I consider this a miracle.

There have been many other miracles in my life. However, it never occurred to me to make a special note of them. I accepted them as gifts from God. I am not a very religious person in the conventional sense. I attempt to observe most of our Jewish holidays and I honour God. I am, mostly, a very spiritual person.

A miracle, then, can be far more complex than the event itself. Sheila was given a car. That, in itself, is not a miracle. What makes the experience special is that at the precise time she desperately needed a car, one was provided by a comparative stranger, given for no other motive than that he wanted to give Sheila what she most needed. Most unrepeatable offers come with conditions higher than Everest. It is perhaps a sad comment on the modern world that such gifts are so rare in times of need as to be regarded as miraculous.

~ *Miracles in the world of business* ~

Can miracles be wrought in any sphere of life? Can there, for example, be miracles in the world of business where wheeling and dealing are more common than divine intervention?

David, who lives in Dorset and is now a healer, sent me the following experience that suggests there may be:

> Late in 1971, I moved from a rented factory to a newly built freehold factory near Alton in Surrey. This was a challenging step to take since it meant that, in order to cover the cost of a newly acquired mortgage (I had been paying a peanut rent for some 20 years), I would have to raise my turnover some 300 per cent. Achieving this was a miracle in itself and confounded my sceptical accountant.
>
> I entered 1973 with confirmed optimism. Business continued to expand and staff had to be engaged. Again my sceptical accountant warned me not to overstretch myself, reminding me in the same breath that I could not continue for long if trade slackened. I would quickly drift into bankruptcy. I remained confident. I had my 'out of the world' contacts. They really worked for me.
>
> My company's major purchase was a few tonnes of extruded plastic sheets per annum, these being converted into a variety of products. These materials were purchased exclusively from British manufacturers and were essential for us to continue production.
>
> During the autumn of 1973, my mind was heavily engaged on a project in my workplace when a thought popped into my mind. I tried to dismiss it but it was no good. I had to stop what I was doing and step into the office. I began rummaging in the filing cabinet and found the subject of my thought. The previous year a representative from a Norwegian company called on me to introduce his company and their range of extruded plastics. It was this company's brochure that I had retrieved from my filing cabinet. I studied it, then telephoned the agent's office in London and ordered 2 tonnes of material for delivery in January 1974. This was the very first time I had placed an order with a foreign supplier and there was no reason to be discontented with my usual supplier.
>
> The early days of 1974 heralded the national fuel crisis. Only three days in seven had power. The delivery

> times for extruded plastic from all British suppliers escalated overnight, from six weeks to six months. However, the 2 tonnes ordered from Norway arrived mid-January and kept the factory operative on a profitable basis until the fuel crisis was over, even though we were restricted to a three-day working week. Without it I would have been ruined.

A hunch or inspiration from David's 'other-worldly sources' whom he believed helped him many times? Are we all capable of tapping into 'other-worldly sources' or, as I prefer to view it, into a source of collective wisdom? Many small firms, run by caring bosses, did go into liquidation as a result of the fuel crisis. Was the difference that David had learned to listen to and trust the inner directions that ran counter to logic?

The miracles in this chapter have been rooted in the everyday world. The next chapter, however, involves experiences of other dimensions, from pre-birth to beyond the grave. But even here, the miracles are described by men and women with feet firmly on the ground, who have spontaneously encountered worlds sought in vain by philosophers and dreamers through long years of study and meditation.

8

Transcendental Miracles

Man is not merely a creature of the here and now. Evidence suggesting that life continues after death, and may begin even before birth, provides some consolation when we are faced with seemingly unanswerable questions about death and bereavement. Miracles indicating that those we love can remain with us after death, and protect us in times of danger, offer the greatest hope and yet attract the harshest denial by sceptics.

Protection from beyond the grave

Julia's experience echoes many I have discovered in the course of my research and suggests that her late husband is with her, not only in memory, but in actuality, as her special guardian.

Julia, who lives in Essex, wrote to me after reading a book I had written on family deathbed experiences called *Families Are Forever*. Her husband Adrian had died in 1988, aged 22, of leukaemia:

> The previous year, my late father-in-law, whom I'd loved dearly during his lifetime, came to me while I was pegging out washing in the garden. He was standing in the

kitchen doorway. He gave a half-smile and said, 'Adrian's got to come to us.' Though his words were gentle they were firm. Then he was gone.

Adrian was fit and well at the time but over the following year he declined and became terminally ill. As Adrian lay dying, unconscious and heavily drugged, the nurses warned me he was totally unaware of me or what I was saying. But when I had a minute alone with him, I leaned over and said, 'I love you.'

Instantly Adrian's eyes opened and he said in a strong, clear voice, not at all confused, 'I love you too.'

Though he had not opened his eyes in hours, in that moment they were open and Adrian's soul or spark was looking out at me. I felt a warmth and Adrian suddenly called out, 'Dad'.

He held his hands in front of his eyes and said, 'The light.' Adrian was pointing to the corner of the room. All the hurt had left his face. I had a strong vision of a vacuum in the room, like a black hole but with brilliantly shining lights.

In our short married life we had a very close bond. Was I experiencing a small part of what Adrian saw as he died?

Two years passed and I was not coping well with his loss. One night I had a dream. It was and still is so clear you could touch it. It was the top half of Adrian. His hair that he had lost during chemotherapy was black and glossy again. He had gained weight and wore a shiny black leather motorbike jacket, an item he had never owned. There was a thin mist around him and he said, 'It's OK. My blood's still a bit dirty but they are looking after me.'

Adrian was gone and I remembered that was the way he described his illness once when he was alive and the treatment was going well. I told my family but they said I must forget and move on.

Some years later I met a lovely man. We married and I had a beautiful little boy. One morning, I suddenly felt I must go up to my son urgently and I ran upstairs. As I

> opened his door, Joss had climbed out of his cot, somehow climbed up to the bedroom window, opened it and was sitting on the window sill.
>
> I panicked but realised that someone was holding him safe. I saw shadows of arms, gripped round Joss tightly. Joss was laughing but not moving. I took Joss out of the unseen arms, carried him to safety and only then thanked Adrian who had saved my child from almost certain death.

Even those who insist such experiences are coincidence or wishful thinking would be hard pressed to explain how Julie's son was held safe, unless they ventured another explanation equally unacceptable to sceptics – the sheer power of a mother's love to protect a child who is in danger far away.

~ *Messages from beyond the grave* ~

For those who do not see or hear a loved one after death personally, a message or sign may come from someone close, usually a child, because children can cross dimensions as easily as they skip across a garden. Sheila, who lives in Lincolnshire, is now in her mid-forties. She described what happened when she was nine years old:

> I was at my grandmother's house. My parents were there, as well as my aunts and uncles. It was usual for them to meet most Saturdays at my grandmother's house.
>
> They were all busy talking. I glanced up from the comic I was reading and saw a smiling young woman standing next to the open fireplace. She was cradling a baby and I have never in my life seen anyone look so radiant.
>
> I was concerned that her dress would catch alight as it was very near the flames. I told her that the flames were near her dress. She smiled at me, put her finger to her lips, shook her head and vanished. The whole family looked at me when I asked, 'Where has the lady with the baby gone?'

One of my aunts suddenly burst into tears. I did not know at the time that she had recently lost a baby, who was stillborn. Children were not told such things in those days. My grandmother looked at me knowingly.

Years later I was looking through my parents' photograph album and saw an old black and white photograph of a smiling young woman. 'That's Florrie, my sister who died when she was 21,' my father told me. I nodded. I already knew who she was, the same woman I saw cradling the baby all those years ago at my grandmother's house.

I believe she was telling me that she was looking after my aunt's baby in heaven. Appearing to a child, she knew I would not be afraid as most adults are. Since that experience I have never been afraid of the after-life.

~ *Deathbed visions* ~

Some of the most moving experiences are from those who have tended dying relatives who have, at the point of death, no matter how ravaged with pain or even incoherent, suddenly become lucid. At such moments, the dying speak of beautiful lights, gardens or even of seeing Jesus. My own mother died from cancer when I was 19 and, as I nursed her in the last moments, her face – which had aged 20 years in a matter of weeks – suddenly became young again and she smiled and spoke to her late father. At the time, I shut out this experience as I did with so many concerning her death and it is only now, 25 years on, that I am able to see the wonder without my personal pain intruding.

Many people, even those who have no faith, at the final moments of their life have either a religious experience or see a loved one waiting. Pamela, who lives in Portsmouth, described her father's last moments:

When my father died about 12 years ago, about an hour before his passing, he eased himself up in his hospital bed, his eyes widened and he was quite obviously seeing something or someone quite clearly and said, 'I'm going

> to Jesus now.'
>
> What is surprising about this is the fact that my father always had very bad eyesight. He wore almost pebble glasses, could not see a thing without them and yet he was without his glasses, his eyes wide open. He always squinted without them but now was seeing something perfectly well without them. Added to this, he was a totally non-religious man throughout his adult life and yet Jesus was the last word he spoke.

Anne, from Lancashire, described how her aunt went to visit her father in the nursing home where he was being cared for:

> He told her about the beautiful lady calling him from the window. My aunt could see no one but, as my father was ill, she thought he was confused. She told me I should go and see him so I went the next afternoon. I held his hand for two or three hours and he told me quite clearly and coherently that his angel was waiting outside the window for him. He died shortly afterwards smiling.

Emma, also from Lancashire, told me:

> Towards the end of my mother's life, she seemed to know nobody for long periods or even who she was. However, my young son insisted on going to see her, although we warned him she would not recognise him. To our amazement, she sat up quite alert and said, 'Hello, Mark, when are you going back to school?' Then she asked me. 'You don't mind if I go over? You've got John and the children.'
>
> I told her she should go when she was ready and she died two weeks later. As she was dying she told me she could see yellow spring flowers, though there were none in the room. She became very excited just before she died, telling me she had already seen her late sister and another daughter, who had died 47 years before, when she was only 20 months old, had come for her.

The above three experiences are only a few of the many deathbed visions I have heard about. All portray an optimism and a consistent assurance that death is no more than a door, on the other side of which familiar faces and love are waiting. I often wonder, when I hear rationalists smugly dismiss the experience as the effect of dying brain cells, if they will have the courage at the last moment of life, when a loving grandparent offers them a hand, to turn the figure away as a delusion.

Not only Christian angels appear at the point of death. In the November 1995 issue of the journal *Sai Reflections*, Susan wrote of the father of a Hindu Sai Baban devotee living in India. As he lay dying, the old man opened his eyes and told his daughter to move to one side, as Lord Garuda, the golden divine bird of Narayana, had come to take him to Vaikunta. She stepped aside and he closed his eyes again peacefully and passed over.

~ *Premonitions of a loved one's death* ~

Another wondrous phenomenon is the ability to link into a loved one's death hundreds or thousands of miles away, even when the death is totally unexpected. Chapter 3 describes several wartime miracles concerning soldiers who returned home either to say goodbye or to assure a relation they were well. In the latter case, even when official news came saying the person was dead, the vision proved to be true and the soldier or sailor returned months later. Whether this is a form of projection by the astral body or, in the case of death, the loosening of the spirit at the point of leaving the physical body is hard to say, but it is a wondrous assurance that love can survive death and is remarkably common.

Pauline, whose healing experience was described in Chapter 1, was living in New Zealand when she linked into her own father's unexpected death thousands of miles away in Scotland:

> For three nights in a row, I dreamed of Canongate, my Dad's old church in Edinburgh. In the dream, there was

a baptism taking place, but the christening gown was empty and the cloister was full of people crying. I knew it was connected with my father and wanted to phone home, but my husband persuaded me to leave it, as my mother would let me know if anything was wrong.

On Tuesday, my daughter Jenny, who was only four, asked me why Grandad Dee had gone to heaven and why was he smoking his 'smogarettes', as she called his cigarettes? I reassured her that Grandad had recently undergone an operation on his lungs but that he was fine. Minutes later, my mum phoned to tell me that my father had died suddenly, two days earlier on the Tuesday, but she had not told me as she had not wanted me to drop everything to fly back when there was nothing I could do.

John is a radio presenter living in the West Country and has often given me a hard time when I have tried to justify my belief that there is some psychic or spiritual bond that exists beyond the body, operating through the channel of family love. So I was surprised when he told me:

I was living in Lyme Regis and my grandfather was ill in Newcastle-upon-Tyne, several hundred miles away. I was worried and was making arrangements to go and see him but, at 2am the same night, I woke and heard loud gunshots.

Next morning a phone call came to say my grandfather had died during the night. When I went home for the funeral, I asked my mother the time my grandfather had died but she was not sure. I said that I thought it was 2am. Before I could explain my reasons, my father said, 'Yes, I think it was 2am. That was the time I woke and heard loud gunshots.'

Alex, who lives in Essex, explained how his mother believed a childhood pact had been fulfilled. Indeed, in Chapter 3 he recounted how his mother saw her brother at the point of death while he was in the Army in France:

As a girl, my mother Kitty became friendly with another lass of about the same age named Maria. They discussed the possibility of life after death and made a firm pact that whoever died first would make every effort to return and let the other know that she had indeed survived death.

Time passed and their paths parted, mother eventually hearing by letter that her friend Maria had entered a convent. Some years later, my mother woke during the night, aware that someone was in her bedroom. She rubbed her eyes and in the darkened recesses of the room stood a figure which then moved slightly forward into the light coming through the window. Mum stared in surprise as she beheld her friend Maria in her nun's habit. Maria said nothing but smiled and vanished. Afterwards my mother heard that her friend had died. The pact they made all those years before had been honoured.

~ *Dying well* ~

The time spent moving into another dimension at death can, I believe, vary from a few seconds to weeks or even months. Roy Castle, actor, trumpeter, comedian and television presenter, died from cancer in 1995 after a long illness. His widow Fiona described how, during the ten days before his death, Roy seemed to move into the next dimension through a series of visions of a beautiful garden and brilliant lights that resembled none he had seen on earth. Finally, the last time the pastor gave Roy holy communion, he saw Jesus standing at the doorway. Roy died with no fear of death and did not blame God for his illness. Instead his faith became stronger and he and his wife were baptised into the Baptist Church three months before he died. Roy believed that God wanted him to use his suffering to help others with the disease and, indeed, he was in the public eye, fund-raising and continuing his message of hope almost until the very end.

Catherine, who lives in Cheshire, told me of her mother

Norah's angelic vision which occurred not at the point of death but months earlier when it became clear that her illness was life-threatening. The experience removed her mother's dread of dying and eased the passing not only for Norah but for all who came in contact with her. The experience is not verifiable for only Norah saw the angel, but those around witnessed the miraculous change in her.

Many will see such a visitation as a sign that there is a heaven and that angels may really answer prayers. However, even if one regards Norah's experience as symbolic (and angels with golden wings are our mind's perception of an abstract eternal spirit of light and goodness), its message is no less wondrous in asserting that we need not fear death for we are and always will be part of that light.

Catherine wrote:

> My mother was a practising and devout Catholic all her life but had always been terrified of dying and going to hell. This fear took hold of her when she became ill and kept growing.
>
> A few days before Christmas 1991, Mum was told that she had a large tumour on her brain and that her condition was very serious. She went into the Manchester Royal Infirmary on 26 December and was given a scan. The tumour was much bigger than had been thought and without major surgery she would not live. However, there was concern about whether my mother would survive such an operation. She was very frightened. But suddenly she confronted her fears and they were gone.

Before her death, Norah gave an account of her vision on 27 December:

> It was late at night. I was completely alone and it was dark and very quiet. I started to pray for all my old friends, people I had not seen for a while. As I prayed, I pictured their faces before me. Suddenly their faces changed and they became horrible, like gargoyles or

those terrible masks that people wear at Hallowe'en. They were sneering and leering at me and I said, 'Oh, St Michael, protect me.'

He came with the faintest of sounds like the softest of sighs. I wasn't in the least bit frightened. He was so beautiful, about 8 foot tall, with ash blond hair, just above his shoulders. He was wearing a full-length gown, edged at the neck with gold, and the colour of the gown blended into peach at the hem. His feet were bare.

St Michael was not at all feminine. He was so strong but with the most beautiful face I have ever seen in my life. In his hand he held a magnificent sword, enormous and very heavy, yet he raised it as though it was no heavier than a feather. He wielded the sword from side to side and the evil faces disappeared. He never spoke to me but, when the faces were gone, St Michael gestured to me with his hand to go behind him and then he opened his wings slightly. The feathers were like the softest down and cream, edged with apricot. He closed his wings around me and I knew I was safe. Then he was gone but since that night I have never been frightened and I have felt full of peace.

It was a wonderful experience and it was real. I know that if I ever need protection again he will come. If anyone is in trouble or afraid, pray to St Michael. He helped me and will not let you down.

Catherine was amazed by the transformation:

The morning of the operation, we went with my mother to the operating theatre. She needed no pre-medication. She smiled and waved to us as we left her. She survived the seven-hour operation. The brain tumour was found to be malignant and we were told there was nothing more to be done. However, after her experience with St Michael, she never again knew fear. Mum died on 9 April 1992. I was with her every day. There was a peacefulness and sweetness that had not been there before.

> Everyone who saw her came away enriched. She told her story to everyone she knew. It never altered. She reached a point where she was able to say, 'I'm dying and I'm happier than I have ever been in my life'.

Some might say St Michael, if he had really been St Michael, could have performed a real miracle and healed her tumour and that he was no more than a malfunctioning part of her brain that projected the vision. It is hard to understand why some people die – good, kind people who have never said a harsh word or done a mean deed, why innocent babies of loving parents should be found dead without warning. These are questions that will not go away.

Yet it *is* miraculous that a woman's fear of death, a fear many of us can never bring ourselves to examine, was defeated and that she died with faith and peace. The hardest thing is to see the miracle and yet not lose sight of the sorrow, the fact that Catherine lost a beloved mother who suffered prolonged pain. The faith shown by Norah and Catherine is an inspiration to others who are afraid of the curse of mortality, of simply ceasing to be, which the psychologist Erich Fromm saw as mankind's greatest burden. It is a miracle I personally need to believe.

There are those who insist that such moments are merely physiological processes as brain cells cease to function. But no one can scientifically replicate the process of dying or know for sure what lies on the other side. Simulations involving hallucinations or drug-induced states miss the immensity and intensity of death as the gates between the dimensions open up.

~ *Near-death experiences* ~

Over the last few decades one of the most productive areas of such research has been the near-death experience, when those who momentarily die during an operation or illness leave their bodies and travel through a dark tunnel to a point of light where angels or deceased relatives may greet them. It is an area I have studied in depth and I have discovered that the most significant aspect for those who have experienced NDEs is usually their homely quality. For the guide waiting at the end of the dark tunnel is not usually St Michael or a being of light but a familiar Mum or Gran, waiting to send the bewildered person back to the world with a smile and a hug. Those people I have interviewed have found this personal contact at the gates of heaven immensely reassuring and, more than anything else, it has helped to remove the fear of dying. Even so, we should not overlook the miraculous nature of leaving one's body, touching death and returning, not unchanged but knowing that death is not the end.

I met Adam, who is 30, when I was working for the cable television station Wire TV and he was demonstrating the Sinclair C5 'racing car'. Adam actually shared his father's near-death experience:

> My dad was in hospital for a minor operation, but he had a bad reaction and at 3.10am he blacked out. His heart temporarily stopped and he momentarily clinically died. I knew nothing of this but at 3.10am I woke up suddenly with an incredible feeling of lightness.
>
> I was halfway out of my body when I felt my father slipping away. I was willing him to pull and to fight and was pulling with him. After about 20 minutes I went back to sleep.
>
> When I visited my father early the next day, I told him of my night-time experience and he spoke to the nurse who showed me the record of the time he had died. He was a forthright thinker, but he told me that, as he was dying, he knew I still needed him and his help and so he had pulled himself back. He was 64 at the time.

I am indebted to Peggy Mason, editor of the *Sathya Sai Baba Quarterly* magazine, for the following near-death experience which was sent to her by a reader, which concerns Sai Baba himself, the Indian holy man whom many Westerners as well as Eastern devotees believe to be God incarnate on earth. Rose explained:

On 1 November 1995, my son Ben went into hospital. It was a relatively minor operation but it was expected to be quite painful for a few days. Ben is a 14-year-old autistic boy and it was difficult to make him understand what was going to happen. I tried to explain and he was fairly calm when he eventually went to the operating theatre. I was told that he would be in theatre for about an hour.

By the time Ben came back to the ward, after nearly three hours, I was getting worried, but he seemed fine and recovered quickly from the operation. We came home the same evening and, although I was told Ben would be very sore and possibly very sick, he slept well all night with only a little discomfort.

The next day Ben was watching television when he suddenly started talking about 'being a ghost'. He can use only limited language and uses a mixture of speech and sign language. I asked Ben what he meant and he said that when he was asleep during the operation he had become a ghost.

Ben told me that he was looking down from the ceiling and saw himself lying on the table as the doctors operated on him. He said the doctors were wearing masks and green gowns and he was lying with his eyes closed.

Then he described going through the wall to a place like a big cloud. There he saw Sai Baba who welcomed him and materialised *vibhuti* [sacred healing ash] which he sprinkled over the site of Ben's operation. Then Ben described his grandmother's dog, also called Ben, who had been put to sleep 18 months previously. Ben said the dog was now 'new' and was jumping up so excitedly at Baba that Baba told him to sit. The dog had been quite old when he had passed over.

Ben then said he saw the 'taxi lady'. She had been the escort for the school taxi and had died very suddenly just before Christmas last year. Ben said she was very happy and hugged him and told him to be a good boy. Then he mentioned another lady with eye glasses who turned out to be his great-auntie Annie who had died two years ago.

Ben then saw the doctor tapping him on the arm, telling him to wake up. He went quickly back into his body and woke up. Ben does not usually display any emotions but, as he was telling me about his experience, he kept wiping tears from his eyes.

Four days later the nurse came to our home to remove Ben's dressing. She was amazed that the incision had healed so completely that he no longer required a bandage. He has recovered very well from the operation and has experienced very little pain.

We are very grateful to Sai Baba for taking such loving care of Ben and giving him the 'out-of-body experience' so that he could share his vision of Baba's omnipresence with us all.

What was so remarkable about Ben's experience was that, because of his limited ability to communicate, he would have had little idea of the significance of what he had seen and certainly could not have created a classic NDE. Sai Baba appeared instead of the traditional being of light, but to Ben and his family Baba is God and so the inexpressible was made more comprehensible by clothing the being of goodness in the terms that to them represented divinity.

Children's near-death experiences are particularly remarkable in that they are so pictorial and mirror the adult experience enough to overcome any suggestion that the idea is a learned cultural one or the result of childish imagination. Near-death experiences can also have profound effects for years after their occurrence.

Gary was seven and living in Ryde on the Isle of Wight when he had a tooth extracted:

The dentist administered too much gas and my heart stopped. I went into a very dark tunnel towards a point of light. It was like sitting on a train going fast. I was mad on trains when I was young and so I was not in the least scared. But as I reached the light, I heard a voice saying, 'It's all right. He's going back.'

I completely forgot about the experience. Everyone said it was just a dream. Then 20 years later, in 1990, I was lying down in the dark with a migraine and I felt someone holding me down and pressing my head. I felt something wriggling inside, as though hands were inside my body, moulding me into a new shape. The pressure on my head ceased. The pain was gone. The next day I opened a Bible and from that day I turned to Christ. Three days later, as I was praying, I remembered my childhood experience and knew it had really happened and that I need never fear death, for I had seen beyond it.

~ *Birth experiences* ~

Death is one side of the coin of human existence. Birth, too, can offer glimpses of other dimensions, though many of these experiences are also dismissed, put down to drugs administered during childbirth or to lack of oxygen. Yet I have researched this subject for several years and have come across amazing experiences that closely mimic the near-death experience even when no drugs have been administered and when the mother is in no danger of dying. When a woman does momentarily die while giving birth to a child, death and birth collide and she may see angels, lights or simply rise above her body and witness the birth.

One of the strongest reasons for returning to life from death is when a woman has just given birth and needs to care for her child. She may stay near the scene, refusing to move towards the light because of her child, torn between life and death by her love for an unborn infant. The near-birth experience is one of the most exciting aspects of this phenomenon, where birth and death become one and the child pulls the mother back to life.

Evelyn, a writer and broadcaster who lives on the South Coast, momentarily died during the birth of her daughter:

My daughter was born on 7 May 1950 at St Mary's Hospital, Portsmouth. She was eight weeks premature. I had been under observation during the previous months, as I had complications including heart problems. In those days medical matters were not as advanced as they are today. Most of the treatment consisted of bed rest and diet. I make a point of this, as the amount of drugs was minimal. I had been in labour, after an induction, for over ten hours and was no longer having bearing-down pains. It was decided to use forceps. At the moment of decision, I seemed to fade back into space and then I heard a voice say, 'We are losing her.'

The next thing I knew I was up in a corner of the labour ward, looking down on someone lying on the bed. The figure looked very small and tired and I realised it was me. 'Poor old Evelyn,' I thought and watched in a very detached manner at all the hustle going on around the bed. I saw the baby born on the next bed and put into a blanket. I'd lately become very friendly with the mother in the next bed and she verified what had happened exactly as I had seen it. I heard a voice saying, 'Go back, Evelyn. We are not ready for you.'

I then felt a rushing wind which seemed to pull me down to the floor and then a voice saying, 'Come on, Mother, you have a lovely daughter.'

My daughter Sally weighed only 4 pounds and was in danger herself. She was rushed away to an incubator. During all this time, I had no drugs or anaesthetic, except when I was stitched. The outcome was even stranger when I went for specialist advice later. I was told that no heart condition was now present.

I told no one of the experience, apart from the other mother. In those days you did not talk of such things.

Clarrie's life was not in danger but she saw an ethereal being in those magical yet frightening moments after birth:

I gave birth during the last war, just after I had been evacuated from London. I woke suddenly. There was a

> moon and it was not dark and facing the window was the figure of a man wearing white – his head was slightly bent back as if in prayer or on sentinel duty. As I looked in astonishment the figure dissolved before my eyes, leaving a wisp of white that looked like a cloud. It was about 12.30 in the morning.

It seems that, in spite of all our modern technological wizardry, we understand as little about the mysteries of birth as of mysteries of death. Through the child, the mother is able to glimpse another world.

Peggy, who lives in Kent, described her own magical birth experience:

> I was 48 when our son was born. During pregnancy I had a dream of seeing my son in full colour aged about six months, the image of how he turned out to be.
>
> Having had a double broken pelvis, it was thought better for me to have a Caesarean, with an epidural, as I wanted to be awake. Immediately after the birth, that wonderful obstetrician Sir John Stallworthy lifted my baby, saying, 'Your baby boy is born.'
>
> At that, I heard a great burst of music like a *Te Deum*, fantastic. Music continued in my private room when holding my son Gavin. Both of us used to hear music, I am sure, for at such moments he too listened avidly. At last I asked the nurse what was upstairs, the place from where the music came. She looked at me very oddly and said, 'Nothing. This is the top floor.'
>
> When Gavin was two days old I had an astral projection in full colour. I found myself in a lovely L-shaped room, panelled, with casement windows looking out on to sweeping grass and trees. Though I could not see him because of the shape of the room, my son was talking to me in a grown up voice. After a time, I asked him, 'How is it possible for you to be talking to me like this when you are a newborn baby?'
>
> Gavin replied: 'I can talk to you now because I am not yet fully attached to my new body.'

I then got a bit apprehensive about some sparkling coloured lights and whipped back into my body through the top of my head. I only wish I could remember what he was talking about.

He was the most angelic child, never a night up, always happy and with a lovely singing voice and he has always, from those first days, loved music.

When, then, does the child's spirit first exist? Does it already exist, as some people in the West as well as the East believe, waiting for a body in which to be born or reborn? I used to doubt the idea that the child's spirit could exist in another dimension. However, I have received many accounts of this pre-birth world and encountered young children who have described past lives, giving details of concepts they could not possibly have known about using words not previously in their vocabulary. I am increasingly convinced that there may be profound truth in it. But only rarely have I heard of mothers who have seen this 'higher self' before birth. Such manifestations raise questions about the nature of our essential being – whether, as Wordsworth suggested, 'our birth is but a sleep and a forgetting'.

Sue, who lives in San Rafael, California, believes that her son Joshua's own higher spiritual essence protected her even before his birth and that he was a wise being who came to teach Sue and her husband truths beyond measure:

Shortly after Joshua was conceived, both myself and my husband felt very clearly that the baby was a boy and his name was Joshua. We sensed he had been waiting a while to be conceived. At 22 weeks, I went into active pre-term labour and almost delivered Joshua. By this time I had already been hospitalised for a week and doctors stopped the labour with drugs after a very intense night. The next morning I woke and saw three beings of light. I don't know how else to describe them. One was over my husband who was sleeping next to my bed. One was over my head and the third over my belly for the baby. I clearly felt each one was there to take care of us.

After about three weeks in the hospital on complete bed rest and an IV drip of magnesium sulphate for the pre-term labour, I was very depressed that my natural pregnancy and birth plans were ending this way. I was told I would have to stay this way for the remainder of the pregnancy, three more months. Going to sleep feeling sorry for myself and scared for Joshua, I felt the most wonderful presence fill the room. It was like nothing I had ever felt before. It was all love, goodness, light and peace. I felt the presence surround me and enfold me in itself and I went to sleep feeling so comforted. I knew it was Joshua's higher self. It was not Joshua, the baby within my body, but rather who he was beyond his human body – his essence, soul or eternal being, which was beyond humanness. I wish I could describe it better but can't since the realm beyond our body is one with which I am not readily in touch.

I was fortunate enough to feel this presence the same way one other night. My husband was delighted and because of this incident we gave Joshua a Seneca Indian name, Hokseda, which means among other things, Higher Self.

When Joshua was born he was relatively healthy but had to stay in hospital for two weeks. When separated from him, I would send him all my love in the form of pink light and envelop him with this loving light. His caretakers used to remark on his peaceful nature. Many a night we would try to leave when he had gone to sleep but, as soon as we walked towards the door, his eyes would open and stare after us. It broke my heart but no matter how late it was I would go back to his bassinet and stay until he went to sleep.

A few weeks ago, I was going to sleep and, although he was in his crib in his room, I felt his spirit on top of me. I had been thinking of him and how much I loved him when this happened and I knew that he was always going to be part of my husband and myself and would always be with us in spirit if not in body. We feel blessed that such a special soul has chosen to spend his life with us.

~ *Astral travel* ~

The Aborigines believe that their *mekigars*, or 'clever men', can travel astrally in spirit form even during life, remaining connected to their earthly bodies by an aerial cord. Such an ability would indeed be miraculous. There are accounts in more developed societies of these 'living ghosts'. Strangely enough, such astral forms can be seen by a third party, when the astral traveller is unaware of his or her walkabout. This would suggest that the spirit or essence which is at its most fluid and free at the points of death and birth – Peggy's baby son told her he could talk to her because his spirit was not yet fully attached – can also leave the earthly form at times of personal distress. These events are very different from deliberate attempts to induce astral projection, which often fail precisely because the emotion and need that prompt spontaneous astral travel are absent.

Simon, who lives in Sevenoaks, Kent, described his out-of-body experience:

> It took place one weekend in the summer of 1994. My mother and grandmother went out shopping on Saturday. After a full day out, they returned to my mother's house. My grandma lives a few doors away. My mother's house is very unusual, as it has a very large round window about 7 feet in diameter, and beyond this window is the living room with full view of the furniture. My mother's house also has a driveway where she parks her car. As she lives by herself, she parks the car in the same place each time.
>
> On this day my mother and gran drew up to the house and saw me sitting in the living room. I got up, walked to the front door and opened it to let them in. This was seen by both my mother and my grandmother and they returned from the car, both asking, 'Where is Simon's car?'
>
> They walked through the doorway to find I was no longer in the sitting room. They searched the house calling me and were very upset when I did not answer.

My mother telephoned me at home, only to find no answer. Later that afternoon I did go to my mother's home. It was the day I split up with my partner after being together for three years. I returned to my mother's house for a roof over my head but I had not been there earlier.

Occasionally a living ghost can appear not to a relation but to a friend or neighbour. This occurs if a person has no close family but suddenly makes a silent cry for help. In this case, a receptive person can unconsciously answer the call and perhaps bring comfort to the wandering astral form. Tracey lives in Redhead, Australia. She experienced a living ghost, a friend who had no one else to care for her:

In 1987 I was living in a one-bedroom flat with my two-year-old son, and Sue, my next-door neighbour, was a married woman who was separated from her husband as he had physically abused her. Periodically she became depressed, feeling that the failure of her marriage was her fault. Sue had dinner with me one evening and sat talking until about 10pm. As she left she said something strange, 'If you need me tonight call me.'

I thought that Sue was more likely to need me but it was a lovely thing to say. I felt uneasy that night and locked all the windows and the door very carefully. I don't know what time I woke but I know that I had been asleep because I was in the middle of a dream about my old school. As I woke, I saw standing in the doorway a white faceless figure and I knew at once that it was Sue from next door by her shape. Just as I was about to ask, 'However did you get in?' she floated over my son's bed and through the wall to her own flat. My son stirred from his sleep as she passed over him. I lay in my bed terrified, thinking that if that was her ghost she must have died and there was no way I could help her. I did not know what to do – I just lay waiting for morning.

I had to go out early the next morning and when I returned Sue was being taken away in an ambulance. She had overdosed in the early hours but had been found by a visitor in time. She survived and started a new life for herself. When I told her about the experience she did not recall coming to visit me while she was unconscious.

Did Sue, as she drifted from life towards death, call in actuality for Tracey because she regretted taking the overdose? Finding her call unanswered, did she then leave her body? Or did she visit Tracey before she took the overdose? Sue did not at any point clinically die but she was in that strange half-state between dimensions. Tracey did not realise Sue's danger on a conscious level and yet perhaps she did offer comfort to the wandering astral form. In a fictionalised version, Tracey would have realised her neighbour was in trouble and rushed next door and saved her. But in real life we are beset by uncertainties, afraid to listen to signs from other dimensions, hesitant to intrude, to follow an instinct. Wondrous powers have their drawbacks for sometimes they tell us what we would rather not know or prompt us to act without hard evidence. That is why the world of the psychic should never be treated as a party game or conjuring trick. The human psyche is itself miraculous but, if we are to utilise more than its most superficial aspects, the moral responsibilities are immense.

As we have seen, the power of love lies behind many of the transcendental miracles described in this chapter.

The next chapter looks at further examples of miraculous devotion, of partners or parents who have cared for loved ones for years without reward and who have at last won through, and of those who have given their lives for others less fortunate. These are accounts of ordinary people who have displayed extraordinary patience and endurance.

9

The Power of Love

The ties that bind

Family devotion, whether that of a parent or a partner, is frequently taken for granted. Yet miracles, large and small, occur daily in such contexts, often overshadowed by the startling events that make front page news. Most of us know someone who has made a willing sacrifice for a family member or partner in need, perhaps over years or even decades. There are rarely immediate rewards. Yet such people are touched by an inner radiance that shines through their exhaustion and sorrow. They are the true miracle workers.

Having studied the power of the maternal instinct, I have discovered that it is not a one-way process and that even a small baby can exert a powerful pull on his or her mother's psyche. As has been seen in several accounts in this book, where a patient is in a coma, the devoted presence and stimulation of a loved one can trigger quite remarkable recoveries. One of the most moving accounts is that of an infant whose love dragged a mother back from the grave. In June 1991 British newspapers carried the story of Caroline Head, an 18-year-old mother of a child in Bradford, northern England, who had been in a coma for two months after falling 25 feet down some steps at a club in the city. Doctors had warned that she might never regain consciousness because of the severity of her head injuries. But her mother, Mrs Christine Wilson, regularly took Caroline's 13-week-old daughter Danielle to the hospital and kept putting the child in Caroline's arms although she was unconscious.

Mrs Wilson told reporters:

> I also played tape recordings of Danielle crying and gurgling all the time I was with her. I was hoping Danielle might reach Caroline in a way the doctors couldn't. Then Caroline suddenly opened her eyes and asked: 'Can I hold my baby?'
>
> It is a miracle that it has worked and just goes to show the bond between a mother and her baby.

Sceptics can argue that there was nothing 'magical' about this recovery. Doctors say that the presence of family or friends in the same room as a patient in a coma can sometimes bring about a recovery because their sounds, smell or feel somehow penetrate the fog surrounding the victim's brain. But the child did rouse the mother in a way that medical science could not. Love was without doubt the key to her recovery.

Such love does not exist solely in the mother/child relationship. Roxanna, who lives in Kansas, displayed a devotion to her desperately sick husband that, in terms of time and endurance, goes beyond the demands of any marriage vow. It is perhaps significant, in view of the previous account, that the care Roxanna offered was like that of a devoted mother for her child.

Lonny, a refrigeration repairman, was diagnosed as a manic depressive in 1971 and for the next 11 years received intermittent residential care in ten different psychiatric institutions. In 1982, he felt, and indeed appeared, entirely cured and therefore decided to stop taking medication. However, during that year, he suddenly fell into a vegetative state. Roxanna was warned that he would never recover and that he should be institutionalised permanently.

Roxanna, mother of nine children, had worked at nursing homes and had seen that by keeping patients moving, deterioration was prevented. Being a lady of immense courage and determination, she refused to accept such a hopeless prognosis and to abandon the man to whom she had promised lifelong fidelity. Therefore she decided that she could and would overcome Lonny's catatonic state by carrying him on her back. This she did by tying his feet to the outside of hers, putting his arms over her shoulders and wrapping his fingers round her waist with a belt strapped to her waist, relying on his reflex action to grip.

Roxanna continued this punishing routine for six hours a day, for five years, talking and singing to Lonny to stimulate his reactions. She carried him as she hoovered, cooked, cleaned, made beds and walked up and down stairs. Roxanna even exercised with him, using simple aerobics, anything to stimulate the reactions that she was convinced were still there waiting to be reawakened.

After 18 months Roxanna discovered Lonny's feet were moving independently, which she saw as a gift from God and a sign that her beloved husband would recover.

Six months later, Lonny spoke for the first time and, after five years, Lonny was able to walk and talk again. Lonny is now fully recovered and is on the board of the hospital where he was once a patient. He and Roxanna run Spirit, an organisation to help the homeless and mentally ill build new lives. Lonny has no memory of the five years that Roxanna carried him.

Dr Stephen Feinstein, a leading psychiatrist at the hospital in Ottawa, Kansas, where Lonny was once a patient, considers that it was Roxanna's devoted actions, rather than spontaneous recovery or mere chance that stimulated the inner recesses of Lonny's brain.

Roxanna, who had to endure a great deal of mockery and scepticism, succeeded because of her persistence and love for her husband. It was these qualities that enabled her to continue, especially in the first bleak 18 months when her efforts seemed in vain. As Christine, the coma patient in the first chapter pointed out, life is rarely like the story in which Sleeping Beauty awakes and instantly recovers. The real miracle is the devotion of family members who refuse to give up and whose faith is justified. In an age where life is sometimes valued cheaply, Roxanna is a reminder that miracles are made by human as well as divine angels.

I met Melissa, a film producer from Santa Monica in the United States, when she came to England to make a programme for Paramount Pictures about psychic families. She became an object of adoration for my youngest son Bill and, as we walked through a London park, Melissa told me of her own late mother who had defied the prognosis of doctors to stay alive for Melissa's graduation ceremony. Melissa believes it was only maternal pride that kept her mother going and that it was the love between them on a psychic level that enabled Melissa to be at her mother's bedside to say goodbye:

> My gran, aunt and mom died within three months of each other. I was 22 at the time. My gran lived with us and was 92 but very healthy. My aunt was a diabetic but the disease was under control.
>
> In the spring, my mom developed breast cancer but she didn't tell anyone and didn't go to the doctor. When I came home for the Christmas break of the senior college, she looked pregnant. But she was 50 and she didn't look at all well. Mom refused to go to the doctor.
>
> When I went back on the plane, I begged her with tears in my eyes to go to the doctor for my sake and she promised. But by then the cancer had spread and it was too late. The doctor told my mother she only had a couple of months to live. Mom lied to me and told me she could be cured.
>
> Mom told the doctors that I was graduating in May and that she had to be there. Her doctor told her it was highly unlikely. But Mom went into major remission and attended the ceremony. The following March, my gran died at the age of 92. Mom was talking to me four times a week on the phone because we had a really close relationship. I sensed something was wrong but Mom said she was fine and Dad told me she was just tired. But the feelings of deep unease kept returning. Three weeks before Mom's death, I woke up after a dreadful dream, sobbing. In the dream, I got a phone call at the house I shared with three other people now I was working. In the dream I was alone in the house and the call came

from our next-door neighbour back home, which was really strange, telling me my mom was about to die. In the dream I could not make it to the airport in time. After the dream, I phoned home and Dad assured me everything was fine.

My mom died exactly three weeks later. I was working on a shoot in Redlands, California, and it was 110 degrees. I was on my own, driving back through the desert. All the way I felt urgently that I had to get home fast. It was a nightmare journey and the air-conditioning on the car broke down. No one was there. I tried to calm down and cook dinner but I knew I must call home. Mom and Dad had regular times when they were at home. Mom worked on Tuesday and Friday nights but this was Wednesday and they were always there. I phoned my best friend to ask if she had seen my mom. My friend had seen her the week before and she was fine.

At this point, the operator bleeped to interrupt the call and it was my next-door neighbour back home, just as in my dream, and not my dad as I would have expected. She told me Dad had gone to the hospital with Mom and that my mother would not last the night. I screamed and sobbed as I had in my dream. I said I was getting a plane straight away but the neighbour said I would not make it. I insisted I would. I phoned my office at 7 o'clock at night. It was strange because a guy I worked with, whom I didn't know that well, who never worked late, was there that particular night.

'Can you drive me to the airport?' I asked him and I explained about my mom. He drove at about 90 miles per hour all the way and got me to the plane just as the doors were closing. I was allowed on. I got to the hospital at 6am the next morning. Mom held on for me and died at 9am. She was getting distressed, saying, 'I don't know what your Dad will do about clean shirts.'

I asked the nurse to give my mother some more morphine. I said, 'You can let go now, Mom,' and it felt like a huge whoosh, as she finally let go of life. It was weird, hard to describe, like a sudden shift from one dimension to another. Her doctor came into the room and I said, 'My mom hated doctors but she loved you.'

I found I was telling people what my mom wanted them to know, what she would have said. I went back to work three or four days later. It was as if I was my mom for two weeks. I usually didn't like the food she ate but I found myself enjoying it. Two or three weeks later I had a dream. I was at the airport with my mom and dad. My mom had bare feet and was sad. Dad and I had to leave her and go off on a plane. The strange thing was, we were leaving her. After the dream, it was as if all the psychic links ceased and she had left me.

Melissa's mother waited to die until her daughter came. Another surprising factor is that Melissa's aunt and grandmother also died within three months of each other. I am convinced that such close deaths result from an enduring love whereby a husband does not wish to live without a wife or a mother a daughter. June, from Leicester, described her parents' devotion which meant that even death was unable to divide them:

My father died only a few months ago. My mother died two weeks later. I was very distraught, then a few days later I looked through the window into the back garden and saw both my mother and my father walking on a beautiful stretch of grass. Both holding hands, looking much younger – and he had been blind and crippled.

I contacted my brother Harry who lives 10 miles away. He immediately said: 'I know what you are going to say. You have just seen both mum and dad walking on the grass. I have seen them too.'

Another case I heard about involved an elderly man and woman who died within two hours of each other. They had always said that they could not live without each other, but most surprising was that the couple were in different hospitals and the husband, who was not seriously ill, had not been informed of his wife's death.

If such devotion can prolong life, then one wonders how many people simply turn their faces to the wall and die because they have no one to care. I encountered a nurse who said she had witnessed this in geriatric wards. The current boom in psychotherapy and counselling is, I suspect, less due to the desire to release hidden traumas than to simple loneliness and the longing to be cared for by another human being.

One of the saddest and yet most inspiring situations is when an elderly partner cares devotedly for a sick husband or wife, even when their own health may be failing. Such care continues day in and day out, with only the scarce resources of community health care to provide practical relief. It is even more tragic when the sick partner is not only failing physically, but losing his or her memory and mind. I was sent this account by a partially sighted and deaf gentlemen, whose cheerfulness and courage stand like a beacon:

> My name is Sidney and my wife's name is Doris. We are both 80 years of age. My wife has been failing for about two years and she has been taken about in a wheelchair for about 12 months. I had a summerhouse built for her, which she thoroughly enjoyed, fully lighted and heated, and we spent many happy hours there both day and night.
>
> One very cold frosty night in February 1994, Doris decided to have a walk to the summerhouse. I was asleep curled up under the bedclothes. Suddenly out of nowhere I heard three distinct staccato calls of 'Sid, Sid, Sid'. I shot from beneath the clothes, out of bed, through the door to the hall, round the room to the door, into the hallway, through the kitchen and the conservatory on to the patio, all in my bare feet, to find Doris stretched out with her face to the ground, feebly calling, 'Sid'.
>
> How ever anything escaped from her lips to me through the space from the patio to the bedroom has always seemed a miracle to me. If it had not happened she would have perished in the intense cold.
>
> When I reached her, I turned her over and around, made her crouch her legs and then I got behind her to

drag her backwards. As I lifted, I told her to press with her feet. It worked, only 6 inches at a time, until I slipped on the ice and hit the back wall with my head. I can still feel the impact of the bricks. I did not stop. I do not know how I continued, but I knew if I did not my wife would not survive. We continued up a little step, through the back door into the conservatory where we rested on an American rocker. How I got her on to the chair I do not know. This done, I washed the blood off her face, cut a strip of plaster and bound the cut over her eyebrow.

God was certainly with us that night. I shall never forget the staccato calls that I could not have heard with the human ear, as she could barely whisper, or the strength I was given to lift her.

~ *The kindness of strangers* ~

Devotion to those we love is understandable, but it is harder to believe that there are those who risk their lives for people they do not know. Altruism has become unfashionable. The desire for personal gain, publicity, or the assuaging of unconscious guilt, are frequently used to explain selfless acts. However, few could doubt the sincerity of those who daily put their lives in danger to save others.

One hero who risked and lost his life was John Bradburne, an Englishman who looked after lepers at their settlement in Mutemwa during the Rhodesian War in the late 1970s. Charles Moore, now Editor of the *Daily Telegraph*, produced an article for the *Sunday Telegraph Review* on 28 August 1994 on John Bradburne, based on his own extensive knowledge and research. Mr Moore has allowed me to reproduce part of his article to tell the story of a man considered by many to be a saint of modern times:

> Fifteen years ago, the war in Rhodesia was at its height. The white Government still kept all main roads open, but the guerrillas of the Patriotic Front controlled much of the hinterland. Whites in outlying areas were told that

the authorities could no longer protect them and were invited to move to safer places.

By August 1979, there were only two white men left in the area of Mutoko, a trading post about 70 miles from Salisbury [modern Harare]. One was Father David Gibbs, a Roman Catholic priest at All Souls Mission. The other was John Bradburne. On the night of 2 September, Bradburne vanished from the round tin hut that was his home. In the early hours of 5 September, Father Gibbs found John Bradburne's body beside the main road. He had been shot.

John Bradburne was born in 1921 into the High Anglican English upper-middle class. In the war he was an officer in the Gurkhas. After the fall of Singapore, he and one brother officer had to live for a month in the Malayan jungle before managing to escape. Later, he served in Orde Wingate's Chindits. During the war he began a lifelong friendship with his fellow Gurkha John Dove, later a Jesuit priest, who is the main guardian of his memory.

People who met him would have quickly discovered that he was humorous, musical and eccentric. It would have dawned on them more slowly that he was profoundly different from most of humanity.

To the question, 'So what do you do?' which the world always asks, John Bradburne could provide no satisfactory answer. He had a few brief jobs – forestry, schoolmastering – but it was clear that his mind was elsewhere. He was searching for God. In 1947, he converted to Roman Catholicism. In the ensuing years, he tried to become a monk, twice in England and once in Belgium, but gave it up. He fell in love and came close to marrying. He made a penniless pilgrimage to Jerusalem, wandered round England as a species of minstrel, became caretaker of the Archbishop of Westminster's country house in Hertfordshire, and, while living for a year in southern Italy, made a private vow to the Virgin Mary that he would remain celibate. He was clearly holy but, equally clearly in the eyes of many, hopeless.

When he was nearly 40, Bradburne wrote to Father Dove, by this time a priest in Rhodesia, and asked him if he knew of 'a cave in Africa which I can pray in'. He came out and joined his old friend. Even there, he did not really settle. Although he worked happily enough on various mission stations, and loved the people, fauna and flora of Africa, he did not find a niche. 'I'm a drone,' he would say. He felt superfluous.

One day in 1969, almost a decade after Bradburne's arrival in Africa, his friend Heather Benoy, who used to play the guitar to his long recorder, suggested they go to see the leper settlement at Mutemwa, about whose poor condition she had heard. They arrived to find a scene of dereliction. The lepers were dirty and hungry, their sores suppurating, the roofs of their tiny huts falling in. 'I'm staying,' said Bradburne and, being him, he meant it literally – that he would stop there and then, and for good. Heather Benoy pleaded with him, eventually in tears, until the sun began to set. At last he agreed to go back to Salisbury to collect his few belongings, but on the journey he said, 'Damn you, Benoy. You know I've got to stay.' He went straight back to Mutemwa and remained there for the rest of his life.

John Bradburne became the warden of the settlement, and gave the lepers the care they had never had before. He improved their hygiene and housing, driving away the rats which used to creep in and gnaw their insensate limbs. He bathed them himself, cut the nails of those who had fingers or toes, fed them, and cared for them in sickness. He knew them all and wrote a poem about each one of them (there were more than 80). With his encouragement, a small round church was built at Mutemwa, and Bradburne organised the music for the Mass, playing Bach on a harmonium and teaching Gregorian plainchant to the lepers. When they lay dying, he read them the Gospel.

After about three years, the Rhodesia Leprosy Association, the body responsible for Mutemwa, fell out with John Bradburne. They seem to have had a narrow view of their duties, and felt that Bradburne was extravagant. He was criticised, for example, for trying to provide one loaf of bread per leper per week. And he infuriated the association by refusing to put numbers round the necks of the lepers, insisting that they were people with names, not livestock. The Association expelled him from the settlement.

But he would not go away. He lived in a tent on Chigona, the mountain hard by Mutemwa on which he was accustomed to pray. Then a friendly farmer gave him a tin hut, with no electricity or water, just outside the settlement fence. There he lived for the next six years, and from there he ministered to the lepers as best he could, often by night. He was more or less a hermit, praying long and regularly, writing religious verse, bathing in a pool on Chigona, living completely without money, and wearing the habit of a Third Order Franciscan, which he had been granted. He grew his hair and beard long. He scarcely ate: 'I've always wanted to fly, and I reckon that if I'm very thin I have more chance of doing so' was his characteristic explanation.

John Bradburne is supposed to have told a priest that he had three wishes: to serve and live with lepers, to die a martyr and to be buried in his Franciscan habit. In all the excitement over his death, this last wish was not properly fulfilled. Father Gibbs, who had taken his habit from his hut for safe-keeping, forgot to dress his body in it, and turned up with it at the funeral in Salisbury, placing it on top of his coffin.

Also on the coffin were three white flowers, placed there by a friend of Bradburne's to symbolise his devotion to the Trinity. In the course of the funeral, a Jesuit priest, Father Michael O'Halloran, was amazed to see a drop of fresh, crimson blood fall from the coffin. He stepped forward and placed a cloth on top of it. Two more drops fell onto the cloth. This was witnessed by several others, including Father Gibbs and the undertaker, who was mortified at what he thought must be a failure of his own workmanship. After the funeral, the coffin was opened and the body inspected. It was dry and there was no sign of any issue of blood. John Bradburne was at last dressed in his habit, and buried as he had wished.

The character of John Bradburne's life and the manner of his death naturally gave rise to the idea that he might be a saint, and the story of the three flowers, the three wishes and the three drops of blood added a possible element of the supernatural. A cult quickly sprang up.

People began to attribute miracles and cures to John Bradburne's intercession. These range from the sublime to the bathetic. I have spoken to a woman whose terminal cancer suddenly vanished after her communication with Bradburne in prayer, a man who says Bradburne warned him in a dream about the circumstances in which his son would die, and a girl who says that she got a job in a building society after praying to him. John Bradburne prayer cards are distributed across Zimbabwe.

A steady trickle of pilgrims, black and white, from Zimbabwe and now from many other countries, makes its way to Mutemwa, and they are attended to by a guardian of the shrine who herself claims to have visions of the Virgin Mary. Many connected with Bradburne have strange experiences of being visited by eagles or by swarms of bees, to both of which he was, in Franciscan style, devoted.

However, among those who knew and loved John Bradburne, I discovered sharp division about all of this. Father Dove, the man who knew Bradburne best of all, is unshakeably convinced that most of the signs and miracles are genuine. He believes in Bradburne's sanctity, and in the visions of the woman who guards the shrine.

Many accept this, but a larger number of John Bradburne's friends are uneasy. To them, John Bradburne was a brave and good man and a dear friend, and it feels false to insist on larger claims at this stage. It is too early, they feel, to enter into the formal processes of beatification and santification with their requirements of proved miracles. They respect Father Dove but think he goes too far.

There, for the present, the matter rests. If Bradburne is declared a saint, one suspects that it will be done by generations yet unborn.

On 18 September 1994 Father John Dove wrote a letter to the *Sunday Telegraph* referring to the miracle of the sun that had been seen by group after group of pilgrims at Mutemwa: 'This phenomenon at Mutemwa has been picked up by video and ordinary camera. Some of the pilgrims, including the guardian of the shrine, claim to have seen the Virgin and Child in the sun.'

At a time when heroes tend to be seen as gun-toting two-dimensional television stereotypes, accounts such as Charles Moore's remind us of a nobler world where real heroism may mean washing lepers' feet and fighting for fulfilment of their basic needs. In his youth John Bradburne was noted for his fiery temper and arrogance. Perhaps that is the real miracle, that imperfect human beings can attain spiritual heights because, and not in spite of, their sheer determination.

The next chapter looks at one of the most remarkable holy men of our times, Sai Baba, whose popularity among Westerners is sometimes explained as a 'throwback to the sixties by ageing hippies' and whose miracles are often dismissed as 'conjuring tricks'. However, Baba's 100 million devotees throughout the world insist that he is God Incarnate. What is more, his miracles, cynically said to be a mass media update of Christ's miracles 2,000 years before, have been witnessed not only by those who have visited his ashram, but in ordinary homes. For it is in their homes and workplaces that Sai Baba is said to answer the needs of those who call upon him, in ways that assure them of his presence and blessing.

10

Miracle Man

Sathya Sai Baba is believed by many devotees in the Western world, as well as Asia and Africa, to represent divinity in human form. He himself claims to be the reincarnation of the first of three Sai Babas, Shirdi Sai Baba, a Muslim saint who died in 1918 in India.

Sai Baba's early years

Sathya Sai Baba was born on 23 November 1926 into a Hindu family in Puttaparthi at dawn on a day dedicated to the worship of Shiva. Puttaparthi is a small remote village in southern-central India and Sai Baba has his main ashram near his birthplace. To this ashram, up to two million devotees at a time will come to worship and be fed and accommodated, almost free of charge.

Before Sathya's birth, an unseen hand would play music on instruments in his parents' small house during the night. Soon after the birth, the baby was found with a cobra, the sacred sign of Shiva, coiled around him. The baby was totally unharmed. As a small child, Sathya gave his food to beggars, refused to eat meat and began to perform materialisations of sweets, flowers and fruits. The fruits, even those not in season or not found in the region, were plucked individually at his companions' request from the tamarind, 'wish-fulfilment' tree, growing at the top of a steep rocky knoll. Friends have told how, when challenged to a race up the hill, Sathya would appear at the top of the tree before they had taken even a few steps, surrounded by blinding lights, pillars of fire, even a full moon framed around his face, glowing golden. When Sathya was 14, he declared he was the second Sai Baba in the line of Triple Avatars and the reincarnation of Krishna and he left home to begin his work.

Although Sathya Sai Baba had only elementary schooling and speaks Telugu as his native dialect, those who have visited the ashram report that he can communicate with devotees no matter what their language. He quotes from the scriptures of all the major world religions and speaks with meticulous, technical understanding on medicine, technology, architecture and science to doctors, philosophers, scientists and businessmen. A number of these 'experts', in spite of their initial scepticism and, on occasions, desire to prove Baba a fraud, have given up lucrative careers to do charitable work on Sai Baba's behalf.

In search of the master

One of the more remarkable 'Road-to-Puttaparthi' conversion stories is that of the former owner of the Hard Rock Café chain, Isaac Tigrett. This American Blues fanatic discovered Baba after many years of searching for spiritual fulfilment and eventually sold his multi-million pound chain of cafés to finance the Super Speciality Hospital that was built about 5 miles from Baba's ashram. Situated in the poorest of areas, this hospital provides highly specialised world-class treatment for the needy free of charge. Medical experts from all over the world work for next to nothing to staff the hospital. An airport has even been constructed at Puttaparthi so that the needy from all over India can be flown in for free treatment.

When Isaac was 13 and living in Tennessee, his brother died in his arms. Isaac was so grief-stricken at this sudden encounter with death, he did not speak for six months and dated this as the beginning of his spiritual quest. Even at this stage, he knew that somewhere there was a spiritual master waiting for him.

The family moved to England and when Isaac was 21, on 21 June 1971, he opened the first Hard Rock Café at Hyde Park Corner in London. Its success was phenomenal and the chain expanded throughout the world, making Isaac's fortune. At last Isaac was led to visit India, not to visit Sai Baba, but to study various holy men reputed to have miraculous powers, for a documentary based on *The Secret Life of Plants*, a book on psychic phenomena to which he had bought the television rights.

When he got to his hotel, a voice told him, 'I have been waiting for you. You have come at last.' Isaac realised that the voice was coming from a picture on the wall, of a small man with a shock of black hair, wearing an orange robe, with the most loving smile Isaac had ever seen. Isaac asked staff the identity of the man in the picture and was told that he was a holy man called Sai Baba. Isaac left that day for Baba's ashram.

When he arrived, there was a festival taking place and there were crowds of people waiting to see Baba. But Sai Baba walked up to Isaac and filled the palms of his hands with sacred ash that flowed from Baba's outstretched hand. Isaac knew beyond doubt as he looked into Baba's eyes, although no words were spoken, that he had come home. This was the master he had first sought as a youth. But the path would not be easy. Isaac started to go back regularly once or twice a year, staying as long as two months at the ashram. This he did for 15 years and during that time Sai Baba did not speak or even look at him. Yet Isaac still knew that he was loved and that there was a purpose.

In 1974, Isaac realised his faith had been justified. In California at 5am he was driving down a canyon and fell asleep at the wheel. The car went through a barricade and into a 200–300 foot crevasse. Isaac woke as he crashed through the barrier. The car spun about a dozen times in mid-air and, as it did so, there was gentle pressure on Isaac's shoulder. Isaac was not wearing a seat belt and, since the car was a convertible, he should have been hurled to his death. Sitting beside him was Sai Baba, quite real and solid, with his arm around Isaac's shoulder, holding him safe. The car was completely and utterly destroyed. There was no windshield, no doors remaining, yet Isaac walked away with barely a scratch.

The very next week Isaac went to India to thank Baba. But again Baba completely ignored him.

In 1976, Tigrett received further proof. He was staying in a hotel in Denver, Colorado, when he suffered an epileptic fit. It was 10.30 at night. Isaac lost all ability to move his body. He was hyperventilating and swallowed his tongue. Isaac choked and at that moment his spirit rose from his body. He looked down on his body and felt total peace and floated towards another dimension. But suddenly he realised that it was not time to leave the earth, as there was so much he still had to do. Isaac called Sai Baba's name, asking for help. At once, Sai Baba appeared three-dimensionally, picked Isaac off the floor, placed him gently on the bed and pulled his tongue free so that Isaac could breathe. As Isaac returned to consciousness, he became aware of Baba's shock of black hair and three gold buttons on Baba's robe. At this point, Isaac's spirit returned slowly back into his body.

Once he had recovered, Isaac again went to see Sai Baba to thank him but again he was ignored. It was not until 16 years later, after Isaac had finally talked with Baba, sold the Hard Rock chain, and financed and organised the construction of the Speciality Hospital (which, from a piece of waste ground, was open to perform its first operation within a year) that Baba mentioned the incidents. Isaac was standing with a group of distinguished architects and doctors when Sai Baba commented almost as an aside, 'I saved your life twice, didn't I Tiger?'

~ *A religion of love* ~

It is significant that Sai Baba does not court either the influence or the money of the rich. Isaac had to wait more than 15 years before Baba would even speak to him. Indeed, Sai Baba often seems to pick a humble peasant or housewife for an interview, leaving the wealthy and renowned waiting.

Now 70, Sai Baba declares that he is here only to serve mankind. He teaches that God is everywhere, there is divinity in everyone, and that all life is sacred, whether animal, human or vegetable. He insists that 'there is only one religion, the religion of love, there is only one caste, the caste of humanity, and there is only one language, the language of the heart'. He encourages devotees to follow their own religions and refuses to accept money for himself, insisting that all donations are made to one of his charities. Remarkable clean water projects and medical care for the poor have been created in very short periods of time, with Sai Baba himself sometimes leaping on to recalcitrant machinery, instantly igniting it to life and joining in the manual labour. The students in his universities dig ditches, serve the poor and tend the cows.

~ *The protection of Sai Baba* ~

But this chapter is not a tract on behalf of Sai Baba. In fact I originally had no intention of writing a chapter on Sai Baba at all. I have never felt any affinity with Eastern culture. What has convinced me that this is an area worth examining in detail is that Sai Baba, whose name means both divine father and mother, represents a very personalized God form to his devotees. They believe that he is with them, not only in spirit but in actuality, wherever they live and whatever they are doing. I have talked to devotees from different backgrounds and cultures. All have the same deep conviction that Sai Baba concerns himself not only with life-and-death events but also with their everyday worries and will help them if only they call on his name.

Whether Sai Baba is God incarnate or simply a very holy man, thousands of his apparent miracles have been recorded by devotees. Are these miracles, as some suggest, part of the natural human desire to make sense of fate? Or are they the acts of a divinity who concerns himself with the daily lives of devotees and non-devotees alike?

Marian and her husband George, who live in Essex, have taken aid to many areas of Europe in need. Marian is a Sai Baban devotee. Like Tony, whose account of his work with the 'Convoys of Hope' is included in Chapter 4, Marian feels that she is protected on her dangerous missions by Sai Baba. It is easy to imagine that such pioneers are immune from fear.

Marian told me of her most recent trip to the Ukraine in March 1996:

> For some reason I was feeling particularly apprehensive about the journey. The night before we were due to leave I had a vivid dream about Sai Baba. Normally I do not remember my dreams but this was so real. I was at his ashram and was angry because Baba had overlooked me, although he had called all my friends to his presence. I protested at his neglect and he put his arm round me, hugging me close. Baba was laughing and his face was so filled with love, I knew he would never desert me.
>
> In the morning all my fears about the trip were gone. The journey was bitterly cold, through snowy, frozen wastes. We were travelling through the wasteland between Poland and Russia, 900 kilometres of deserted military road, no houses, no buildings, nothing but the empty road before and behind us. Suddenly a lorry driven by two of the girls jackknifed on the black ice and turned over. We were helpless. Then, from nowhere, a Russian Rabbi appeared, followed by a van full of Russians, none of whom could speak our language. The Rabbi organised the men and they righted the lorry as though it were a feather instead of many tonnes of metal. The girls were totally unhurt, the lorry was completely driveable and even the delicate heart monitor equipment was undamaged. The Rabbi and van disappeared as though into thin air on that straight deserted road and I thanked Baba, as I had done many times, that he was with us.

But it is not only those on vital missions whom Sai Baba protects. Chloe, who lives in Middlesex, told me:

> In my car I keep two photographs of Sai Baba, one on each side of the dashboard. One evening, as I was driving

down a narrow winding country road, the photograph on the right jumped out into the middle of the dashboard. It continued to move quickly in front of my eyes – it was the picture of Sai Baba with his hands raised. I realised he was telling me to slow down, which I did. Thirty seconds later a car came straight at me at high speed and I was able to make an emergency stop and avoid a head-on collision. A few days later, at the same spot, there was a very bad accident. The pictures were wedged and have never moved at all before or since. Now I thank Sai Baba every time I pass the spot.

~ *Sai Baba's signs of blessing* ~

Many religions have great shrines where visitations and signs of divinity have manifested. In this book I have mainly concentrated on signs of blessing that have appeared to ordinary people, often in their own homes. The following events occurred in a modest terraced family home and continued over a period of three years, in a multicultural neighbourhood of shops, houses and small factories. Had such signs occurred in India, in a grand temple, they would have been hailed as a great public miracle. Bhupendra, an artist, told me of the experience he had witnessed but, because the family concerned wish for anonymity, I have not used their names or given the location of the shrine:

It was 26 October 1986. The bedroom in the house was, the family told me, filled with a dazzling light. There was a lovely fragrance everywhere. A picture of Bhagavan Sathya Sai Baba in the room was materialising *vibhuti*, a white sacred ash possessing healing powers. Sai Baba frequently materialises *vibhuti* from his palms for devotees. *Vibhuti* is the name given to the sacred ash traditionally associated with Lord Shiva. Worshippers of Shiva as well as Zoroastrians adorn their foreheads with the ash as it is symbolic of ultimate reality, since it cannot undergo any further change.

The *vibhuti* was materialising in between the glass and Sai Baba's photo. It was the beginning of a long-term phenomenon.

When I visited the house myself, not more than an hour later, I can hardly express the wonders I saw, the sacred ash slowly rising, almost covering Baba's head. I could not stop my tears. The room was still filled with fragrance and we lit a flame lamp, like a candlestick. My eyes, however, were fixed upon Baba's picture and I was praying, 'Oh Lord, do not cover Baba's head with *vibhuti*, so that he may breathe.'

I phoned several of our Sai Centre devotees and some came to see the marvel with their own eyes. We prayed, sang and chanted the glories of the Lord and Sri Sathya Sai Baba in that room and invited Dr Dhirubhai Gadlua, a very old and well-known Sai devotee. He is full of wisdom and love and has started many Sai Centres in Britain and abroad. He came three days later and witnessed the manifestation of *vibhuti* on Baba's picture. He changed the bedroom into an altar. He performed sacred rituals, bringing Lord Ganesh, Lord Shiva and several goddess statues, and advised the family to offer flowers, food and milk at the altar. He also advised them to keep the flame burning night and day.

After three days of the manifestation of *vibhuti* on Baba's picture we saw an *Om* sign written with *vibhuti* on the wall by the altar. *Om* is the most sacred word for Hindus. For them, it is synonymous with the supreme Godhead, the impersonal as well as personal God. The materialisation of these signs had increased to seven within three days and in a few more days to 108 on the wall. People from far and wide came to visit the shrine to pray and experience God's love, expressed through increasing fragrances of different kinds and a light that grew in intensity round the altar. Devotees also started to bring their own beloved gods' and goddesses' pictures to be blessed by Baba's miracle. Some who left their pictures found they were also materialising *vibhuti* and *kum-kum* [sacred red powder]. *Kum-kum* is used for ritual worshipping ceremonies and as a symbol of earthly love. Married Hindu women use *kum-kum* to decorate their foreheads to express their love to their devoted husbands.

Every day more and more people were coming to the house to pray that their problems might be resolved. On their departure they took with them sacred ashes that now were materialising in piles on every deity and on almost every god's picture.

I began to visit the shrine almost every day. I used to sit silent in meditation for long periods with tears of love in my eyes and I never wanted to leave the place. Visitors came to the shrine from many faiths, Hindus, Sikhs, Christians, Jains, Muslims, and so I had Jesus's picture framed and placed there.

Next day, Jesus's picture also began manifesting *vibhuti*, full of wonderful fragrance. I then put a religious symbol of Mohammed's picture of Ka'bah, the black holy stone in Medina. I was happy to see so many faiths represented in the shrine.

One night after I finished my work and went to the shrine I met some of Baba's other devotees. About ten of us started singing *bhajans* [sacred hymns and chants], beginning with Lord Ganesh's song. We became so engrossed, meditating and singing *bhajans*, that we felt we were in heaven with all the gods and goddesses. After some time, a spark of light sparkled through my half-closed eyes and, as I opened my eyes, I saw a rain of rice grains falling from the ceiling on to the carpet beside us and upon us. All present witnessed the beautiful white rice grains and we thanked Baba with all our hearts for the holy rice grains, as we call them in our Hindu custom, because we carry out a ritual worshipping ceremony using rice grains.

Weeks were passing and the shrine sometimes looked very active and some days there were no phenomena. Christmas was coming and we saw one day shortly before Christmas that a cross with *vibhuti* had appeared on the wall and before long *Om* and cross symbols had spread to the other two walls. Some were disappearing as others appeared. There were 100 *Om* and cross signs in all at one time. The deities of Lord Shiva, Lord Ganesh and the goddesses were manifesting more and more *vibhuti*, also *chandam*, a yellow sandalwood powder. *Chandam* brings mental peace and places a ceiling on desire. *Kum-kum* was also appearing on the pictures. We decorated the shrine with Christmas lights and decorations. Every day we used to offer fresh flowers and also we made garlands to put round the pictures. I was inspired by Bhagavan Baba to paint an oil portrait of him and to keep it in the shop for my customers to see. I put it on the shop wall for several weeks.

On Christmas Day we had *bhajan* singing and chanting the name of Jesus and the names of all the deities at the shrine. There were about 70 devotees in a small sitting room downstairs. We also made another shrine temporarily, with pictures of Jesus and other divinity forms, and I took my oil portrait of Baba to display in the shrine. When we had almost finished our *bhajan* singing and other ceremonies, we noticed manifestations of *amrita*, an oil-like sweet substance, sacred nectar, dripping on my picture. The picture had no glass on it and the drips were clearly visible. All the devotees witnessed this blessing on my painting. The chanting ended about 10pm and next morning I went to the house and my portrait of Baba was now manifesting nectar continuously. I put off any idea of taking the portrait back to the shop. The number of devotees was increasing every day, some as far away as Scotland and other parts of the United Kingdom. On average 20 or 30 devotees came each day and were cared for by the family in whose home the shrine stood.

They came to be blessed and to be healed of their physical pains and mental sorrows. We gave them *vibhuti*, *kum-kum*, etc, and now small bottles of nectar. It is tasty to drink as well as healing.

Not only devotees but non-devotees came, more and more people reporting back that they had been cured by *vibhuti*, even those suffering from forms of cancer and other potentially fatal diseases. The nectar phenomenon continued for about two years, as did the appearance of *vibhuti* and red and yellow powder. The family offered hospitality to all who came, but would not accept any donations or any offers of food or fruits for the altar.

The house formed the nucleus not only for religious signs of blessing but for many healing miracles. It would be difficult even for sceptics to dismiss these experiences as coincidence or fraud, for the events were not only witnessed by many people but occurred over a long period of time. The multi-faith aspect of the phenomenon and the widespread healing shows that divine blessing is not exclusive.

The problem is that, in trying to understand miraculous happenings in materialist terms, an experience can be doubted and denigrated in a way that can be hurtful to those who have shared what was for them a wondrous event. There are no tools that are sufficiently sensitive to 'measure miracles' – perhaps there should never be.

Dr Bhagavantam, a physicist and former Director of the Indian Institute of Science and a devotee of Baba, once commented of Sai Baba's miracles and those who doubted them:

> Science cannot claim to explain everything in creation. Certain things science can explain. It can deal with the material world and can study the properties of matter with the help of five senses, the sense of sight, smell, touch, taste and sound. But there are so many things beyond the senses, for example, love, hate, compassion, the love of a father for a son, liking and disliking. We cannot understand such things with science. We cannot measure them with our eyes, nor sense them with our noses, nor hear them with our ears. Science has its limitations. The miracles Baba does in great number do not lend themselves to treatment by scientific methods, logic or knowledge. Science was developed essentially to study the material world. Miracles are beyond the material world.

~ *Miracles witnessed by non-devotees* ~

Although people of many faiths were involved in the miracle described above, it is sometimes argued that of course Sai Baba and his 'calling cards' will be seen by whose who believe in him. However, the following experience concerned not a devotee but an outsider and took place in Newbury, Berkshire, during 1994. Joan described the incident which occurred before the meeting she was organising for Sai Baban devotees from around Britain:

> On Friday, 4 June, my husband Richard and friends, Navin, Bala, Pat and myself, visited Downe House School, the venue for the Sai UK Newbury weekend, to finalise the accommodation plans. We had used the Centre the previous year for our meeting. Jim the caretaker had kindly shown us all around the school, which is a maze of rooms in the old building. We were talking together when suddenly Jim asked if the man in charge would be here again this year.
>
> We asked whom he meant and he said hesitatingly, 'The man that you – um – worship'.
>
> We thought Jim was a little confused and explained that Sai Baba lived in India and did not leave that country. Jim then asked, 'What about the other one, the old man with the beard?'
>
> We asked if he meant a devotee called Tom, to which he quickly said, 'No, I know Tom well. I mean the old man in the white gown with the beard and a hat like a bobble cap without the bobble. He carried a stick.'
>
> We were now looking at each other, realising that Jim seemed to be describing the late Shirdi Sai Baba. Richard had a picture in his pocket of Shirdi Sai and Sathya Sai Baba standing side by side, the former and present incarnations. Richard showed the picture to Jim who smilingly recognised the old man, saying, 'Yes, that's him. I can remember him so clearly, such a loving face, where does he live?'
>
> 'Well actually, he's dead,' we replied.

Jim repeated, 'But I saw him. This is weird.' Then he asked, 'What about the other one, the other one in the picture?'

Richard said, 'You mean the one in the orange robe with the black hair?'

Jim quickly answered, 'I saw him too. The old man in white was standing in Reception when a car drew up and the next thing I saw was the man in orange standing at the top of the steps before going through Reception into the main hall.'

We were all smiling, realising what a blessing this was, but poor Jim was looking very unnerved about the whole thing, especially as there had been no photographs of Shirdi at the previous 1994 weekend.

We explained that Swami, as we call Sathya Sai Baba, had been seen like this in many instances, which the public at large might find unusual but are everyday occurrences in Sai Baba's life. On arriving home, I asked Richard if he would phone Jim to see if he was all right and also to get the facts absolutely clear without any extra embroidery or memory lapses. Jim was pleased to speak to Richard and told him he could not stop thinking about it. So when he arrived home he had told his wife who replied that she remembered him coming home last year to tell her that the man in the orange robe who organised it all had just arrived in a car.

The caretaker, who handled many different gatherings during the year, had been convinced that the two Sai Babas were simply other organisers and had not seen them as any different in substance from the other devotees who had turned up. There are many stories of Sathya Sai Baba and, more rarely, the previous incarnation being seen at gatherings around the world. One woman even saw Sai Baba in an orange robe moving at great speed in the booking hall of a London Underground station.

Another miracle involving a non-devotee was described to me by Roy. It concerned his friend Bai who owned a factory in North London. Bai was buying a larger factory not far away. Contracts were exchanged and Bai had to clear his factory of fitments by Monday morning. Bai found a lorry to move the machinery and equipment to the new factory on the Sunday morning. However, on Saturday morning, Bai heard that the lorry had broken down and new parts could not be obtained until Monday.

Bai's solicitor warned him that, under the terms of the sale, anything left in the factory on Monday morning would become the property of the new owner, an absolute disaster for Bai who would lose his means of production. It was too late to make another booking and Bai was very short of ready cash, having put everything into the new factory. He asked various friends with vans to see if some of the equipment could be moved and they promised to help as much as possible. Bai was very despondent, as he knew the heavy machinery would have to be left. Then, out of the blue on Sunday morning, a total stranger with a lorry and crane turned up and said, 'I understand you have a problem. I will help you.'

The stranger offered to move the fitments. Using a heavy rope, he pulled the machinery out and, with the crane, loaded it on to his lorry and took it to the new factory. In the confusion Bai forgot to give the man a plan of where everything was to go but when he went into the new factory, to his relief, everything was in exactly the right place. Bai's friends were very suspicious and warned Bai that he was a fool as he had not mentioned money, so the stranger could now charge him a fortune. Nervously Bai mentioned the cost. The stranger asked Bai how much he had in his pocket. Bai only had £70 which the man said was quite enough and disappeared. As the man was revving up, Bai realised he had unloaded his spare tyre in the factory and ran after him. But the lorry disappeared and he was unable to trace him again.

Not long after the move, Bai's wife, a Sai Baba devotee, persuaded Bai to go to India with her to see Sai Baba. Bai was very reluctant, as he was very sceptical of the avatar, but was persuaded to go to the smaller ashram near Bangalore where Baba was staying. Feeling disgruntled, Bai sat in the back row of the *darshan*, hoping it would not last too long. Suddenly a young man came up to Bai and said, 'I have a place for you at the front. Please come.'

Bai was very reluctant to move but did so grudgingly. Almost at once Sai Baba walked past him and Bai realised, to his embarrassment, that Baba was picking up his scornful thoughts. Sai Baba stopped and said to Bai, 'I helped you recently.'

'No you did not,' said Bai indignantly.

'Yes, and you paid me £70. If you want proof you can open a machine,' – Sai Baba described the type of machine and exact location in the factory – 'and you will find the £70.'

Bai was open-mouthed and immediately after *darshan* telephoned his daughter in Kingsbury. The machine was fastened down with several heavy screws and bolts, but there inside quite safe was the £70. When Bai went home, he knew it was the same roll of notes because he had had oily hands when he handed over the money and there were his finger prints. Bai now has a picture of Sai on his office wall and his business flourishes.

~ *God incarnate or a very holy man?* ~

This story seems to provide evidence enough. However, were a single experience to guide me from my own wavering spiritual path to Sai Baba's ashram, it would be the story that Peggy Mason, the author of *Sai, Embodiment of Love* (Gateway Books, 1993), tells of a man who visited Sai Baba in India. Although the devotee knew alcohol was prohibited at the ashram, he brought a small bottle of whisky with him. On the first evening in his room, he poured himself a secret drink but found that the whisky had turned into water.

Next morning Sai Baba walked forward slowly through the crowds of thousands to where the man was sitting, smiled at him, raised his hand as though drinking and said, 'Cheers'.

I do not know whether Sathya Sai Baba is God incarnate or a very holy man who uses divine power to perform inexplicable feats for the good of mankind. A third explanation would be that devotees see miraculous events, like those described above, within the framework of Sai Baba's teachings. But that would not explain why non-devotees have experiences, nor why scientists, doctors and businessmen are prepared to change their entire lives, having once looked into Baba's face. Sai Baba's materialisations at his ashram are often filmed or described on radio or audio-cassettes by eye witnesses. It is hard to imagine suggesting conjuring skills in a similar situation, if the miracle of, for example, Christ turning water into wine, had been recorded on video.

One thing is certain, that Sai Baba's miracles and his teachings warrant serious and sympathetic study, for he preaches equality, peace, the divinity of mankind and above all love, the guiding principle common to all religions and to all who would live a worthwhile life. His devotees are not plaster saints – as in all organisations, religious and secular, there are bound to be quarrels and power struggles. But the vast majority of devotees I have met or with whom I have corresponded or conversed on the telephone, often for hours, are invariably kind and generous. They have lived and suffered in the world before turning to this loving focus of divine love, the one they call their beloved Swami, friend, father and mother in one.

My own experiences concerning Sai Baba have been strange. I was sent a tape of some discourses of Sai Baba by a devotee and my teenage daughter Jade, who has an elaborate stereo system, offered to copy it for me on to one of her tapes. As I played the copy late one evening, my middle son Jack, who is now 11 and started me off years ago on the road to studying psychic experience, remarked on the lovely perfume that had suddenly filled the room. I identified it at once as jasmine. I had not said anything, although I could also smell the fragrance, since I had been told that Baba often identifies his presence through jasmine. I had dismissed the scent as imagination. But Jack knew nothing of Sai Baba. When I played the tape alone a second time the fragrance was gone.

The second experience was even more thought-provoking and, in anyone other than myself, I would have considered it a small miracle or at least incredible synchronicity. As a writer, my financial situation tends to be feast or famine and, with five children, the feasts are rare. My eldest son, who is 17, came into the dining room where I was making notes for this chapter and told me that he had to have £30 that morning to pay for a new battery for his motorbike. He needed it so that he could come home after dark from college, some 15 miles distant down country roads. I said cynically, 'You had better ask Sai Baba for the £30.'

Two minutes later the phone rang. It was the Editorial Director from a publishing company for whom I was not working at the time. He asked whether I would read a synopsis for him and write a brief report to say how it might be marketed. I had not done this sort of work before but asked him the fee. He said, 'How about £30?'

Sai Baba is beyond doubt a man of miracles, while there are others who perform miraculous healings but claim no personal divinity, simply seeing themselves as channels for a greater power. The first account in the final chapter of the book tells of a Japanese teenager who, like Sathya Sai Baba, discovered that his was no ordinary childhood for he was called by the Buddha to become Japan's finest healer.

11

Miracle Healers

The boy who loves flowers

There are those who believe that healing is a natural gift that cannot be taught. Young children are often natural healers but their abilities are lost or become dormant, along with other psychic powers, when they go to school. However, for some, these special skills are reawakened either by a vision or by a life crisis.

In Japan, a 17-year-old senior high school student named Takaaki Moor, rushes home from school each day to heal the sick and distressed waiting outside his door. Up to 14,000 people have consulted him about their diseases and afflictions. Every day, 30 to 40 patients are waiting but he will accept no money at all for his activities. He considers saving people to be his mission. His parents believe that it is their privilege to support their son financially for as long as necessary. Takaaki will accept only flowers which he loves and sometimes fruit. I am indebted to my Japanese friend Atushi for helping me to discover this story and for spending hours translating papers, Takaaki's own book, *I am man of superhuman powers*, and transcribing videos for me. Atushi also sent grapes, the speciality of his own region, to Takaaki by way of thanks for his help.

The story of Takaaki's discovery of his own healing powers has an almost mythical quality. When Takaaki was 11, he received a revelation of the Buddha in Spring 1990. He was reciting the Sutra when a white light flashed out of the family altar. From the light a quiet voice, which he believes was Buddha himself, told the young boy that he would be given superhuman powers and that he had been chosen by Buddha to heal illnesses. Takaaki went into the kitchen where his mother was preparing supper and told her of his vision. His mother would not believe him but at last agreed that if he could cure her painful and persistent headaches then she would accept his words.

Takaaki found that he could see inside his mother's head and that part of her brain was crimson. He prayed that the bad part would be cured. Buddha's voice told him to call out three times for the pain to depart. This Takaaki did. Gradually the crimson colour disappeared and she never again suffered from headaches.

From that moment Takaaki's healing work began, at first with friends and acquaintances of the family, people who were absent as well as directly. For example Mr Yoshi, an acquaintance of his father, had come to the office, dragging his leg and in great pain. Takaaki's father asked for Mr Yoshi's name card, promising that his son would cure the leg by absent healing.

That evening, as Takaaki held the card, a severe pain coursed through his own left leg. When Takaaki put down the card, the pain disappeared. Then, as though on a television screen, Takaaki was able to see an image and realised that the spirit of someone who had died was hanging on to Mr Yoshi's leg. The spirit revealed that he was a good friend who had died but did not want to leave someone of whom he had been especially fond in life. Takaaki explained to the spirit that he was unintentionally hurting his former friend and so the spirit agreed to depart. The pain ceased and later Mr Yoshi explained that he had recently lost a very close friend and had been chief mourner at his funeral. It was soon after his death that the pain had started.

To some Western minds, such a concept might sound strange but there are many ways of expressing the complex link not only between our own bodies and minds but between ourselves and those to whom we are bonded in love. Takaaki explained that at first the Buddha helped him when he did not know what to do, because he was still a child, but gradually his own powers have taken over the healing processes.

In these early days of healing, another acquaintance of his father's, Mr Tanaka, was ill in hospital, suffering paralysis of the arms and legs, caused by a previous back problem. Takaaki saw a middle-aged female spirit who had been killed in a fire 15 years previously when the problem had started. She had clung to Mr Tanaka because she had been in love with him. The spirit refused to go and Takaaki did not know what to do. Suddenly a spherical light came from the sky and wrapped itself around the spirit, carrying her into the sky. Once again Buddha had responded and within a week Mr Tanaka could walk again.

One ability Takaaki frequently demonstrates is to dissolve the energies of the universe and the energies of the paradise of Buddhist souls into ordinary tap water. By drinking this transformed water, the sick can take these energies into their bodies and heal diseases or improve their constitution. Takaaki explains that both the universe water and the Buddhist soul water act in various beneficial ways either upon the body or on foods. The universe water has beneficial effects upon the brain and skin while the Buddhist water is especially effective for problems with internal organs. With foods, the universe water removes dangerous food additives.

Certainly Takaaki's water has been effective in many cases where no other medication has been used. Yamato, a former Sumo wrestler, described how he had become a hairdresser to other wrestlers after he had hurt his wrists and knees and was no longer able to perform. However, he had to use a large quantity of pomade which caused a bad rash, blisters and weeping so that his fingers swelled to twice their normal size. So bad were Yamato's hands, he could not even hold a cup or chopsticks. He also developed swollen lymph nodes and a very high persistent temperature. Visits to hospitals and herbalists had offered little relief and, after a slight improvement, the condition would worsen again. Yamato realised that he would be forced to give up his job.

In March, a Sumo tournament was held in Osaka City. A friend told him that his hands could be cured by Takaaki who was appearing there. Takaaki took a bottle of water, moved his hands over the bottle, let his breath fall upon it and told Yamato that it was universe water, with the healing powers and energies of the universe itself within. Yamato should put the water on his painful hands and also drink it. When the supply of healing water became low, Yamato could simply add city water to replenish it.

After work, the former wrestler put the universe water into a wash basin and dipped his hands in it for several minutes each day. A week passed but there was no improvement. Therefore he decided to dip his working gloves into the water, put on the wet gloves, and put vinyl gloves on top to prevent evaporation, fastening the gloves finally with adhesive tape. He did this every night before going to bed. On the morning of the fourth day, to his surprise, fresh pink skin was showing underneath and the hands gradually recovered. After two weeks Yamato's hands were exactly as they had been and so he was able to keep his job without any further trouble.

It is often argued in such cases that the change in routine or sheer faith makes the difference. Whatever the cause, the dramatic improvement would be noteworthy and Yamato now seems to be protected from recurrence of the trouble, even though he is handling the same chemicals.

Medical evidence seems to support many of Takaaki's cures. For example, a man diagnosed as having a heart problem and high cholesterol levels visited Takaaki who recited the Sutra loudly and pronounced that the heart was now fine and the cholesterol problem removed. When the man returned to his doctor for monitoring, the problem had indeed gone. He had an electrocardiogram before and after the healing.

Many people in Japan believe that Takaaki's work is only just beginning. Until then he puts aside the activities of other teenagers and spends his days answering countless letters, taking endless phone calls and healing the people at his door. He sees only the blessings of his gifts and plans to dedicate himself to the healing of mankind. There are those who will always point to profit or fame as motives. But he appears on television reluctantly and takes only basic expenses. For the boy who loves flowers loves his fellow men, women and children. He believes that he is doing the work Buddha has chosen for him and that he needs no more.

~ *The husband and wife healers* ~

Like Takaaki, Len and Rae believe their healing gifts have divine origins. It is only the name of the deity that differs. They came to healing work much later than Takaaki and were led not by a vision but by their own sorrow and illness. Time and time again, powers, whether for healing or new talents, come not to those who are secure in their own self-worth, but to people who have touched the depths of despair and have emerged spiritually richer and with a desire to help others who are similarly afflicted. Rae explained:

> It was in the early seventies when my husband and I had our lives torn apart in a very traumatic way and our health suffered. My husband said, 'We must start our lives again.'
>
> With his courage and, in spite of the trauma that we were still going through, we did just that. Then I started to have some frightening attacks. They appeared to be like mini-strokes and convulsions, similar to an epileptic fit. I was taken to hospital as an emergency case. A brain scan showed that I had a blood clot on my brain, but the chances of an operation to remove it would involve too great a risk. I was given medication but still the attacks continued. It took some time to recover, as my legs became paralysed and I would lose the use of my hand and arm. My face felt as though I'd had a tooth extracted.
>
> One day I met two healers who saw how ill I was and offered me healing. I accepted their kind offer as at least it gave me hope. However, the attacks returned. I also asked my husband to take me to two other healers, as I was not allowed to drive. Len did this for me but he was

a great sceptic. In both cases the healers told my husband he was the one to heal me. We did not discuss the matter, as my husband was such a great sceptic. Then one day another attack started. I was lying on the bed and my husband took my hand and said, 'Dear God, if I am a channel for healing help me now.'

The attacks stopped instantly and I have never had one since.

Rae also discovered her own healing powers and she and Len have gone on to heal hundreds of patients. Christine, who comes from Bristol, was one of their many patients. She was diagnosed as having cancer. Doctors told her there was nothing they could do, as it had spread throughout her body. She was discharged from hospital on 10 milligrams of tamoxifen and 100 milligrams of morphine daily.

In January 1995, after healing which had made her feel calmer but had not reduced the intense pain, she wrote to Len and Rae whom she had heard had helped many people with all kinds of diseases and on 14 February, after her first visit, immediately felt much better. Christine received healing from the couple at first once a week and then twice weekly, returning to once-a-week treatments until 25 July 1995 when she no longer needed healing. From the first visit to Len and Rae, Christine was able to cut her morphine from 100 milligrams daily to none. The intense pain disappeared and in May 1995 further X-rays were taken which showed that the left and right clavicle and the lungs were clear.

On 22 June 1995, a second hospital report showed that Christine's condition was found to have improved considerably and three months later her doctor observed that she was looking well and radiant. He commented: 'Considering the original diagnosis of disseminated cancer which was made some years ago, her present condition appears to defy medical predictions made at that time.'

Another of Len and Rae's patients, Jim, was diagnosed as suffering from cancer of the liver after a scan and biopsy. He was told that nothing could be done and Jim's wife was told to make arrangements for him to enter a hospice for palliative care. Refusing to give up, Jane put him on a low-fat diet as suggested by the GP. This had to be liquidised because Jim could not eat solid food. Rae and Len gave Jim spiritual healing three times a week and Jane, who was also a member of the National Federation of Spiritual Healers, also gave him healing. Gradually Jim returned to the person he had been before he had become thin and ill. Before long, he regained his normal weight, and he now eats well and can drive a car again.

Jim's doctor could not believe the change in him and asked if he could watch Len and Rae at work, as Jim's recovery was so amazing. Indeed the doctor has since referred more of his patients to the couple.

Further scans showed that the massive tumour had shrunk to less than 30 per cent of its original size, the liver itself was back to normal size and the tumour rapidly disappearing. The GP commented:

> It is a fact that the shrinkage of this tumour is due to the patient having received spiritual healing. I am of his opinion that the spiritual healing caused the shrinkage and that there are beneficent forces available to mankind which can overcome normal physical and biological rules governing the progress of disease.

Other medical research would seem to support the conclusion of Jim's doctor. In 1995, two American doctors, Caryle Hirshberg and Marc Ian Barasch, concluded from their research that the most important aspect of overcoming terminal illness is a person's reaction towards the illness. A determination to recover does seem to bring the strength to do so in many cases or at least to considerably extend life beyond the projected prognosis. A new field of psychoneuroimmunology has emerged, based on the discovery that a positive approach to illness triggers the release of endorphin secretions that activate the immune system towards recovery.

So, are Len and Rae miracle workers? Dr James Le Fanu, writing in the *Sunday Telegraph* in December 1995, noted observations by Dr G.B. Challis of the University of Calgary after an analysis of all the reported cases of spontaneous regression of cancer. He said that the phenomenon has been noted in virtually every type of cancer and at every stage. Dr Challis referred to the case of one woman with cancer of the rectum, in whom it was found at operation that her pelvis was 'so extensively invaded with cancer that only a palliative excision could be attempted'. She lived on for 17 years, and an autopsy after her death reported 'no detectable tumour tissue present'.

Dr Le Fanu, who has made an extensive study of religious and spiritual phenomena in relation to medicine, says that nobody knows why spontaneous regression should occur, but the favoured explanation is that some event, perhaps the trauma of an operation, or an infection, stimulates the production of antibodies that destroy the cancer. Theoretically then, stimulating the immune system in some non-specific way might be beneficial in cancer, and this has subsequently been demonstrated, particularly in treating the skin cancer melanoma.

He sees the importance of recognising spontaneous regression because it can protect patients against being over-treated:

> Cancer specialists have taken considerable pride in the very high cure rate – almost 100 per cent – of the childhood cancer, neuroblastoma, with anti-cancer drugs. Recently, however, it has emerged that when such cancers are left alone, they often shrink to a fraction of their original size, at which point they can be removed with a simple operation.

But Dr Le Fanu does not dismiss the wondrous nature of the phenomenon:

> Anyone witnessing spontaneous regression of cancer cannot help but be moved by what appears to be an almost miraculous event. But in a sense it is just one instance, albeit a remarkable one, of an even greater miracle – the hidden and mysterious ways in which the body sustains and heals itself.

It may be that spiritual healing, as described in Chapter 5, can act as the trigger that Dr Le Fanu speaks of. But those who have faced death and believe they have been cured by Len and Rae, attribute their miraculous recoveries to the loving hands of this particular couple.

~ *The healing lady* ~

Perhaps the strangest story of a healer I have encountered is that of Shirley who seems to have linked into some past life, whether her own she is not certain, of an ancient order of healing nuns. As a result she discovered her own restorative powers. Shirley runs a residential home for the elderly on the South Coast of England. As well as caring for the frail and those suffering from dementia, she offers healing massage to the patients in her care and indeed to all who seek it. The home is warm and comfortable and exudes a spiritual calm, rarely found except in hospitals run by nuns.

Shirley told me the strange tale of how she gained her healing powers:

> During the 1970s I was on holiday on the Costa Blanca in Spain. My husband and I had arrived at Monserrat and intended the next day to visit the monastery that was right on top of the mountains. The night before our trip, at about 3 or 4 am, I woke with a start. The bed was shaking and I heard a voice saying, 'God, the Devil, Redemption.'
>
> I was an Anglican, but found myself responding, 'Redemption'. I saw a figure who was saying the words but I could not understand who it could be. The figure wore a monk's habit, but had the face of a woman, a distinctive pointed face that I will never forget. The cowl seemed velvety soft. Strangest of all I was not the slightest bit afraid. I knew that the figure was kindly and important to me.
>
> The next morning our party went up the winding mountain passes to the cathedral at Monserrat. I lost my husband in the crush and found myself before the most

wonderful, powerful figure of the Black Madonna. A wrinkled old peasant woman who seemed to know me said in English, 'Put your hand on the orb,' and, as I touched the orb that the statue was holding, I felt a strong electric charge tingling through my hand. My husband dismissed my experience as static electricity but it was like nothing I had felt before, a wonderful pulsating warmth and energy. Soon afterwards I discovered that I had healing power in my hands which would become warm and tingling, the same sensation I had received from the statue.

My friend was with us on holiday and she had terrible pain in her arm. Automatically I found myself rubbing it for her in regular strokes as though I was being guided as to what to do. I could feel the tingling warmth leaving my fingertips and she could feel it too. The arm was better almost at once and from then the healing seemed to be always with me.

The experience made such a strong impression on me, and the black and gold statue contained such power, it changed my life. Even the small Black Madonna image I brought home seemed to exude the same energy.

I was working as a nurse at the local hospital at the time but I could not forget the experience, the female monk and the Black Madonna. At last, I went to see the nuns at St Dominic's Convent to see if they could help me. Sister Philomena showed me a Black Madonna statue she had bought from Monserrat in 1949, but was unable to shed any light on the ghostly figure, other than that it might have been a Dominican friar. What he wanted of me she did not know except that such figures appeared to those who had been chosen for some special purpose.

I knew that it was important for me to become a Catholic but I hesitated because I knew that it was an irrevocable step. After two years I was received into the Church. I worked as a community nurse, helping all kinds of people with physical, mental and drug-related problems. I became a Minister of the Sick, taking communion and offering healing and massage to all in need. When I went to Spain I had no desire to become a Catholic nor any knowledge of healing but it was as if, from seeing that vision and then touching the orb, my path was guided and directed.

After ten years I felt impelled to open a home to help elderly people and I am now able to use my healing to alleviate their pain. I took care of Sister Estella, one of the elderly nuns from St Dominic's Convent. It was a problem keeping her habit and wimple starched and there was no money to pay for her, but I knew I must help her as repayment for what I had been given. The nuns were so grateful and I felt I should repay them for their kindness. When the nuns left the area, Sister Philomena gave me her Black Madonna statuette and I keep it with me still.

Some years later, an old lady, Alice, who was 103, died at the home. She had no close relations and so it was my responsibility to clear out her belongings. Among her possessions was an old photograph. I went cold. It was the female monk I had seen all those years before in Monserrat. I had never forgotten that face with the sharp features and now it stared back at me. I turned it over. The woman was Jeanne Jugan, Foundress of the Little Sisters of the Poor, who came from France and who was born in 1792. The cowl was just as I had seen in the vision and I understood that she had been telling me that redemption lay through helping and healing the poor and the sick as she had done.

I continue my healing work and have been able to help many people using the power that was given to me at Monserrat. I recently discovered that the Black Madonna of Monserrat had been found by shepherds hidden in the hills. It was probably brought from France at the time of the French Revolution along with other artefacts, at a time when the Sisters were wending their way down the country towards Spain. Did 'my lady' bring the statue with her? Was I the nun in a previous life? I am determined to go back to France and Spain and follow her possible route to find out what I can.

Shirley would like to open a healing sanctuary for all who need it and feels that her experience in Spain and all the following events are leading her on a path she is destined to fulfil.

~ *The gift of healing* ~

But miraculous healers are not only those who seem able to cure cancers. Many healers, when asking for healing, add, 'if it is right'. We do not know why some people die in spite of healing. The danger is to blame the healer as having failed. Margaret became a healer after her son Robbie became ill with a brain tumour and was admitted to the Royal Marsden Hospital in London. She discovered the power to heal other children but not her own son, who died.

The story of Robbie, who returned after death to play a joke on his mother, is told fully in my book *The Psychic Power of Children* (Foulsham, 1994). In that book she described her experiences of healing with Robbie. When Robbie was very ill, Margaret decided to take him to a psychic healer. As she said, 'at that stage, you try anything'.

> On the way home, Robbie was very quiet: 'You're not going to believe this, Mum,' he said. 'I was lying there. You know the picture of Jesus with the cloak. He was standing there. I looked at his face, He opened his cloak and both my grandads were standing there. I was absolutely terrified and closed my eyes. When I opened them they were still there. It's stupid – why should I see my grandads when they're both dead?
>
> 'She [the healer] put me on my tummy and gradually I was half awake and realised someone had come and put a hand on my back between my shoulders. It was warm. I knew it wasn't Eileen [the healer]. I thought as I had seen Jesus, it might have been him, but that's silly, isn't it?'

Said Margaret: 'I used to put my hands round his head. He said it felt lovely and warm. But I could feel the obscene tumour in his head and I had the feeling I couldn't heal him, though it always made him more settled.'

Robbie's tumour was spreading down the brain stem and Margaret used to take him to a London healer as well, determined to try anything that would help. When Robbie left the healer, he would say: 'The trees are so green, I can see colours again.'

On the Guy Fawkes night after his operation, he said to Margaret: 'Why didn't you tell me that fireworks were coloured?' She realised that for years he must have been seeing in black and white.

But Margaret's own work as a healer was not only triggered by her desire to help Robbie but to help the other children who were suffering. Margaret described her own reaction to Robbie's first healing session in which he saw Jesus in the room:

> I felt enormous electrical, crackling energy bursting through me and the healer told my husband, 'Your wife is a sensitive.'
>
> 'Sensitive, I'll say,' Pete scoffed. He would have nothing to do with the world of spirit. I had no idea what the healer meant at the time. But my healing powers were awakened and I would never be the same. I was at home one evening having a bath and I had settled Robbie down for the night in hospital. I was thinking what a dreadful time two young children in Robbie's ward, who had just received bone marrow transplants, must be having. Their mothers were frantic because the children were at the critical point when they would either recover dramatically or suddenly die. As I sat in the bath at home, I started to pray for them. All I could see was a picture frame and in it the colour yellow ochre and, as I looked into the yellow, I knew I could do far more for the children than pray. I felt a tingling from the top of my head to the soles of my feet, as I had felt during Robbie's healing sessions. I got out of the bath and phoned my aunt Connie who was a healer. 'I want to heal some children but I don't know what to do,' I told her.
>
> 'Go somewhere quiet and ask for healing for the children. Ask a Higher Power to help you,' she instructed me.

I went upstairs and asked for healing for the two children who had received transplants. It was terrifying. My heart started beating so loud and so fast, I felt I couldn't cope with the pounding. I shut my eyes and suddenly found myself flying through the air horizontally. Someone was holding my hand and when I looked I saw a long grey figure dressed in a grey tunic. We landed with a bump outside the Royal Marsden Hospital where Robbie and the two children were. The doors were locked and a gale was blowing a tree on the traffic island where we stood. It was raining but I wasn't wet at all.

The figure went straight through the plate glass doors, leaving me alone outside in the rain. Suddenly I was back in bed. I was totally shaken. I caught a glance at myself in the mirror as I went downstairs – white with two brilliant spots of colour on my cheeks.

'Whatever have you been doing?' my husband asked when he caught sight of me.

I told him. 'Don't you ever dabble like that again, Margaret,' he shouted. But it was the beginning of my real healing work. All night, I was shaking like a jelly and felt a buzzing through my body. In the morning, I felt ill and exhausted and rang my Aunt Connie.

'You did remember to close the healing power down?' Aunt Connie asked and she explained that, after you have been in tune with another dimension, you must give thanks, say amen and shut off your healing powers. After that I felt a thousand times better.

When I used to go to the Royal Marsden Hospital to see Robbie, I would go into each four-bed ward at a time, look at the children and then rush into the washroom, the only private place, and ask for help for them. I never touched them physically. However, one boy called Ian, who was only three, was suffering from a brain tumour. He was becoming increasingly frail. His mother and grandma used to come and see him every day. One day his mother had not arrived and he was a bit upset so I picked him up and cuddled him. I had a strong urge to put my hand between his shoulder blades and massage him. 'Margaret you're burning me, put me down,' he cried crossly. I quickly took my hand away. It was hot.

Later I saw Ian's grandma. 'Did you burn Ian?' she asked me. I tried to explain that I was only cuddling Ian. 'Please go on doing whatever you did,' she told me. 'Ian is so much better.' I explained I had only just started healing and didn't know what I was doing. 'You will learn,' she promised, 'but you must carry on.'

I remembered her words many times during the dark days ahead. The two children for whom I had requested help during my strange out-of-body experience did recover and by the following week had gone home. Had I helped them or would they have gone home anyway? I don't know. I believe, however, that these gifts are granted in times of need and taken away if you use them for gain.

I started contact healing. I was very nervous at first. A powerful force pulsated through me. I couldn't believe the force when I first asked for healing energy. It coursed through me like a flood. Because Robbie was so ill, I didn't have much chance to do contact healing, but I started a book in which I wrote the names of people who needed healing. But even that was more than just asking for help. I would visualise the people before me. Once I asked for healing for a cousin's bad back. I hadn't seen that branch of the family for a long time but my mother had mentioned that my cousin was in constant pain. A very scruffy brown dog jumped out of nowhere into the room where I was working with my healing book. So I healed the dog as well and it vanished. The following week there was a family party and I went with my mother to see my aunt whose daughter had been suffering from a bad back. On the way, I asked my mother if my cousin had a dog.

'Yes, but it's been very ill and they were going to have it put down.'

When we reached my aunt's house, a glossy brown dog bounded to the gate, wagging its tail. My cousin was walking without a trace of pain or stiffness. 'You must have used your magic on Penny as well,' my cousin laughed. 'She's been so much better since you sent me healing. In fact we took her to have her coat stripped this morning. She was really scruffy but we left her, as she was so ill.'

Another friend was ill in hospital with liver trouble. She was given a colostomy. As I asked for healing for her, sitting alone in my bedroom, a little old man appeared from nowhere and walked menacingly towards me. He had a cap on his head. He would not stop walking and came closer and closer. I dropped my healing book and fled towards the door. It had never happened before. Then I stopped. I was not going to be driven away from my work but I realised I needed protection. I opened my husband's Bible at random. The text at the top of the page was 'I will lift up my eyes unto the Lord from whence cometh my help' and ever after I have said those words before I begin healing.

Some years later, I met a window cleaner who was collecting money at a house I was visiting at the other side of town. Out of the blue he said to me, 'I have a message for you. Once you panicked very badly, didn't you, when you were healing, and you were given the words, "I will lift up mine eyes," as a protection? They just want you to know that the protection is given and always will be with you. You must carry on your work.'

Sometimes healing won't work. I knew as I touched one woman that she would not live long. She needed comfort, love and someone to care. I knew nothing would come of the healing so I tried instead to talk to her and listen to her fears.

Ben, a boy of 15 who was very ill, also asked me for healing. As I gave Ben healing, the energies were like a missile rebounding against a metal shield. It just would not penetrate. It broke my heart. Ben was an only child and he was dying. I find it hard to accept that I cannot help in every case, but my aunt says we can't play God. But healing, even if it can't cure, can comfort and help people. What is important is to help people to die with dignity, care and compassion. But why didn't my comfort and love go through to Ben?

You develop your spirituality like a jigsaw puzzle, with a little bit of everything that doesn't make sense until you can fit it in to see the shape of the whole. Clairvoyance, healing, sensitivity, recognising another dimension and coping with it when something manifests itself is all to do basically with our fellow man, whether he or she is alive or has been, an acute awareness of physical and mental suffering and the power to relieve it.

~ *Comfort rather than cure* ~

So healing miracles should not be measured only by whether a cure is achieved. It could be argued that, through David, a businessman, medium and healer, James gained not a cure for his cancer, but peace and freedom from pain that ensured a 'good death'. As with Margaret's early healing experience, a divine being was involved. David explained:

> It was a cold wet November afternoon as I bumped along the unmade track leading to James's little cottage for another healing session with him. James was terminally ill. I had known that since the telephone call six weeks earlier when I was invited to call. For some unaccountable reason I had not seen him for about two years although I heard through the grapevine that he had been ill, hospitalised and had returned home. So it was quite a shock on that first visit to find James so emaciated. Cancer of course. I feared inwardly that James was hoping that spiritual healing, a subject on which I had enthused over the years, would provide the miracle that doctors could not supply.
>
> I called once or twice a week on the way home from work for a 30-minute healing session. I found it initially more difficult working with a close friend. I knew he was expecting so much from me and I felt completely inadequate. As I applied the handbrake that November

afternoon, I let out a sigh, 'What am I doing here? What good is it doing? I know he is going to die and I cannot prevent it. So what is the point?'

As I sat there, drowning in my own sense of inadequacy, a calming influence spread through my body and an inner voice said 'You are expected. You are not alone. You are wrong in your perception. There is a positive benefit.'

I was welcomed effusively by my friend and as I stepped into the role of healer in the warm, welcoming cottage my thoughts were interrupted by the inner voice urging me to close my eyes and relax as I do when meditating and let my mind be clear. In a little while an impression formed. I found myself standing behind James in a room of Oriental decor. A beautiful beaded screen divided the room. The screen parted and a tall, distinguished-looking Chinese gentleman entered, bowed and came towards us. He wore a full-length embroidered cloak fastened at the neck. A small hat, also embroidered, was upon his head. His hands were slender, fingers long and tapering, nails beautifully manicured. He carried gold needles in one hand and I thought, 'Ah, acupuncture.'

As I watched, fascinated, he proceeded to push the needles into my friend's back. The impression faded and I stood behind my friend quietly contemplating what I had seen. Thoughts of a conflicting nature flitted through my mind. Was this a miracle cure? The inner voice prompted me to ask James if the healing was different. He replied: 'It felt as though someone was sticking needles into my back' and so I told James what I had experienced.

I write these words more than 20 years after the event. Yet the impression of that afternoon is as vivid now as it was, all those years ago, of the Chinese gentleman, the texture of his hands and face, an unblemished ivory colour. He conveyed the impression of an elderly person, yet visibly he was not old. The brilliant colours of his garment, his slippered feet, the compassion in his eyes and the splendour of that room were unforgettable. The words, 'You are not alone' returned to me and I felt humbled. My doubt had been conquered by a demonstration that I would never forget.

There was not a cure. James deteriorated. His bed was brought downstairs but after a fortnight he was hospitalised. I had planned to make my first visit to the hospital on Friday evening. But two days prior to this, on the Wednesday, as I was getting ready for work, I had the unmistakable urge to go that very evening. He was in a private ward and my first impression on seeing him was how small he seemed to be in what appeared to be a very large bed. His eyes were as bright as ever. He was smiling and pleased to see me and we shared half an hour together until other visitors came to see him. As I took my leave, he clasped both my hands in his, squeezed them, shook them and looked at me intently saying, 'Keep up the good work, David.'

James passed away within half an hour of my departure, before I reached home. Friday would have been too late. A few weeks later I had a letter from James's widow. In it she told me that when the doctor had come to sign the death certificate, she had questioned the white tablets her husband had been taking. The doctor told her they were not painkillers, but water tablets: 'A remarkable thing really,' the doctor commented. 'Your husband should have been in a lot of pain but he was not. I can't take any credit for that. It belongs to a Higher Authority.'

Those who work miracles, like those who receive them, are not people who exist apart from the real world but people who, often tempered by life's tragedies, use their experience to make the world a better place. They may receive divine inspiration but they know that the miracles are not those of story books but are set against the sorrows as well as the joys of life.

Afterword

'Miracles are the opposite of fate,' my 12-year-old son Jack informs me. 'Miracles make impossible things happen,' adds my eight-year-old son Bill. 'God is miracles,' concludes my ten-year-old Miranda, before they hurtle off in a whirlwind of cereal and crumpled comics to slay dragons in the garden.

Those three statements perhaps summarise the essence of this book, that life is not random. Rather, although I initially believed that all power and wisdom came from within the human mind and psyche, there would seem to be an external power of goodness and light – God, in many names or none. This Godhead can pull us back from the brink of a precipice or blackened dock edge, can enable statues all over the world and from different faiths to drink milk on a single day, can make rosary beads change colour, and a woman return from a dreamless coma lasting more than two years to join in a husband's prayers.

The experiences I have recounted affirm that miracles happen most frequently to men and women living in the real world and that often those who suffer most are most blessed. This is not an attempt to dismiss sorrow or minimise its effects. What mother who has lost a child would not rather hold him or her in her arms than receive a thousand celestial visions? What daughter, recalling her mother's angelic visitations before death, would not barter such religious insight for that same mother's health? We are not given such choices.

Is religion an intrinsic part of miracles? I suppose, in the widest sense, it is. While some who have never been inside a church or temple since early childhood have experienced wondrous events, there is in all those to whom I have talked or corresponded, a deep spirituality, generosity of spirit and kindness. This need not be expressed through formalised religion, but through love of family or country. Indeed there are those who fall to their knees every day of their lives and claim God's direction in their every action who never see beyond their own reflected holiness. Again, those who do not attribute salvation from death or disaster to God, may demonstrate daily in their lives the tenets of any loving religion.

How, then, can we open ourselves to miracles? Life is so busy, constantly, directed towards achievements, possessions, trying to be all things to all people. Even spirituality has become a marketable commodity, with classes, tapes and videos calling us to ever greater awareness and spiritual heights.

Yet miracles are not for sale and the way to discover the wonders of the universe is to stop, to be still. When we look at the sunrise or a rainbow, touch the hand of a sleeping child, see the weary smile of love between an elderly couple, witness a mother in tears of joy at receiving her infant's first hand-made card, we see miracles. Life is a miracle, health is a miracle. Having someone whose face lights up with joy when we return home, whether parent, partner, child or even a pet, is an affirmation that we are precious and loved.

If you have no one waiting, go to a church, synagogue or sacred site at sunset and feel the gentle mantle of love enfold you. Touch a flower, feel the rain on your face and wish on the moon for whatever will make you, not successful, but truly happy. Next morning walk gently through the dew at dawn into the embracing path of the sun and make those dreams come true. Smile at a stranger and, after initial uncertainty, he or she will smile back and pass on the smile. That is a miracle that will go on growing. Whether you are rich or poor, healthy or disabled, in the bosom of a loving family or alone, you too are a living miracle and testimony that each day is full of possibilities. You are unique. That is another miracle and you have your own destiny that will make the world a better place.

I hope that this book will prompt many readers to recall wondrous incidents in their own lives or from their own family histories. If you find the accounts of miracles in this book alien to your own experience of the world, ask family members or friends and you may discover in the attic of someone's mind a half-forgotten memory or family gem, especially from wartime. For the greatest repositories of miracles are not in churches or in dusty seats of learning, but in the hearts and minds of those with whom we share our daily lives. Miracles are, I believe, a consolation for yesterday, an assurance for today and a promise for tomorrow.

Contacting The Spirit World: How to develop your psychic abilities and stay in touch with loved ones Linda Williamson

Creating Sacred Space With Feng Shui Karen Kingston

Energy Connection, The: Answers to life's important questions Betty F. Balcombe

Feng Shui Kit, The: The Chinese way to health, wealth and happiness at home and at work Man-Ho Kwok

Full Catastrophe Living: How to cope with stress, pain and illness using mindfulness meditation Jon Kabat-Zinn

Handbook For The Soul: A collection of writings from over 30 celebrated spiritual writers Richard Clarkson and Benjamin Shields (eds.)

Healing Breakthroughs: How your attitudes and beliefs can affect your health Dr Larry Dossey

Healing Experience, The: Remarkable cases from a professional healer Malcolm S Southwood

Hymns To An Unknown God: Awakening the spirit in everyday life Sam Keen

I Ching Or Book Of Changes, The: A guide to life's turning points Brian Browne Walker

Journey Of Self-Discovery: How to work with the energies of chakras and archetypes Ambika Wauters

Journeys Through Time: A guide to reincarnation and your immortal soul Soozi Holbeche

Karma And Reincarnation: The key to spiritual evolution and enlightenment Dr Hiroshi Motoyama

Lao Tzu's Tao Te Ching Timothy Freke

Life After Death: Investigating heaven and the spiritual dimension Jenny Randles and Peter Hough

Life Signs: An astrological guide to the way we live Julia and Derek Parker

Light Up Your Life: And discover your true purpose and potential Diana Cooper

Living Magically: A new vision of reality Gill Edwards

Many Lives, Many Masters: The true story of a prominent psychiatrist, his young patient and the past-life therapy that changed both of their lives Dr Brian L Weiss

Mary's Message To The World Annie Kirkwood

Meditation For Every Day: Includes over 100 inspiring meditations for busy people Bill Anderton
Message Of Love, A: A channelled guide to our future Ruth White
Messenger, The: The journey of a spiritual teacher Geoff Boltwood
Mindfulness Meditation For Everyday Life Jon Kabat-Zinn
Nostradamus – The Final Reckoning: A year-by-year guide to our future Peter Lemesurier
Nostradamus: The Next 50 Years Peter Lemesurier
Only Love Is Real: A story of soulmates reunited Dr Brian Weiss
Paranormal Source Book, The: The comprehensive guide to strange phenomena worldwide Jenny Randles
Parting Visions: An exploration of predeath psychic and spiritual experiences Dr Melvin Morse with Paul Perry
Past Lives, Present Dreams: How to use reincarnation for personal growth Denise Linn
Past Lives, Future Lives Jenny Cockell
Peter Underwood's Guide To Ghosts And Haunted Places Peter Underwood
Pocketful Of Dreams: The mysterious world of dreams revealed Denise Linn
Power Of Inner Peace, The Diana Cooper
Power Of Your Dreams, The Soozi Holbeche
Psychic Explorer, The: A down-to-earth guide to six magical arts Jonathan Cainer and Carl Rider
Reading The Future: A step-by-step guide to predictive astrology Sasha Fenton
Rituals For Everyday Living: Special ways of marking important events in your life Lorna St Aubyn
River Of Life, The: A guide to your spiritual journey Ruth White
Saved By The Light: The true story of a man who died twice and the profound revelations he received Dannion Brinkley with Paul Perry
Secret World Of Your Dreams, The Derek and Julia Parker
Serpent And The Circle, The: A practical guide to shamanism Namua Rahesha

Stepping Into The Magic: A new approach to everyday life Gill Edwards
Strange But True? Casebook: Amazing stories of the paranormal from the new TV series Jenny Randles
Strange But True? Stories of the paranormal Jenny Randles and Peter Hough
Supernatural Britain: A guide to Britain's most haunted locations Peter Hough
Teach Yourself To Meditate: Over 20 simple exercises for peace, health and clarity of mind Eric Harrison
Three Minute Meditator, The: 30 simple ways to relax and unwind David Harp with Nina Feldman
Time For Healing, A: The journey to wholeness Eddie and Debbie Shapiro
Time For Transformation, A: How to awaken to your soul's purpose and claim your power Diana Cooper
Toward A Meaningful Life: The wisdom of the Rebbe Menachem Mendel Schneerson Simon Jacobson (ed.)
Transformed By The Light: The powerful effect of near-death experiences on people's lives Dr Melvin Morse with Paul Perry
Transform Your Life: A step-by-step programme for change Diana Cooper
Visualisation: An introductory guide Helen Graham
Working With Guides And Angels Ruth White
Working With Your Chakras Ruth White
Yesterday's Children: The extraordinary search for my past-life family Jenny Cockell
Your Healing Power: A comprehensive guide to channelling your healing abilities Jack Angelo

For a free brochure with information on our full range of titles, please write to:

PIATKUS

Piatkus Books
Freepost 7 (WD 4505)
London W1E 4EZ

About the Author

Cassandra Eason is a well-known author and broadcaster on psychic and spiritual experience, folklore and superstitions. Trained in psychology, she is a world expert on parent/child intuitive bonds and a former Honorary Research Fellow with the Alister Hardy Research Centre for Religious Experience in Oxford. Her previous books include *Psychic Families*, *The Psychic Power of Children*, *A Mother's Instincts*, *Families Are Forever* and *Discover Your Past Lives*. She is the mother of five children.